T0128851

GROW YOUR
PROFIT$

GROW YOUR
PROFIT$

CHRIS PROVOST

iUniverse, Inc.
New York   Bloomington

Grow Your Profits
Implement Changes Now to Drive Profit Growth.
Leverage your Marketing, Value Chain, Supply Chain, and
Logistics to achieve continual sustainable green profits.

iUniverse books may be ordered through booksellers or by contacting:

iUniverse
1663 Liberty Drive
Bloomington, IN 47403
www.iuniverse.com
1-800-Authors (1-800-288-4677)

Because of the dynamic nature of the Internet, any Web addresses or links contained in this book may have changed since publication and may no longer be valid. The views expressed in this work are solely those of the author and do not necessarily reflect the views of the publisher, and the publisher hereby disclaims any responsibility for them.

ISBN: 978-1-4502-4418-3 (sc)
ISBN: 978-1-4502-4419-0 (dj)
ISBN: 978-1-4502-4420-6 (ebk)

Library of Congress Control Number: 2010909959

Printed in the United States of America

iUniverse rev. date: 09/08/2010

Contents

To Jesus, my father Herbert, my mother Lois, and my family Estela, Esther, and Ruth—thank you.

Preface

Business strategies for a changing world

In ten years, we have achieved over $200 million in net profit growth for corporations by designing and implementing Value Chain solutions, reducing waste, and supporting environmental stewardship while growing profits. So, is your present business strategy flexible and profitable enough to weather the approaching storm clouds of increased fuel costs, climate change, food issues, and higher taxes? Developing strategic and tactical alternatives is key to preparing your business or government to address approaching disruptive events. Look at the impact a single disruptive business event can have on a company's future. At a Fortune 100 business, we implemented a Strategic Sourcing program, affecting a supplier who had done business with the company for over a hundred years. The supplier lost business they had grown for three generations. This business event required an adjustment in the supplier's cost model. Given the extensive relationship, we gave them months to alter their model, even assigning a manager to work with them, but they could not make the changes required. This resulted in tens of employees laid off and broken family relationships. While we reduced costs, no one was pleased with the structural impact on a company with which we had such an long term relationship. However, increasing shareholder value took precedence, and we could not let a supplier's failure to plan affect our own profitability. If a small event such as the one described can have this much disruption, what will be the impact as the large, macro changes occur?

This book is not *Good to Great*[1] or *Why Smart Executives Fail*[2]; it is about seeing the future and planning for alternatives. Our objective is to help you increase your company's strategic and ecological intelligence[3] so you can achieve a profitable and sustainable social and environmental footprint. This book contains a concise summary of the broad threats and future trends that governments, world organizations, and small and large businesses face. It presents alternative business and government models to aid you in achieving profitable innovations, sustainable growth, and higher margins. The future will require us to take a principled approach to personnel, customers, the environment, and global cultures while applying new cooperative, collaborative approaches to achieve sustainable global growth. The future will increasingly challenge our framework of government and business as we aim for energy-efficient, renewable, clean technologies with reduced water utilization and sustainable food development. The two objectives of this book are to provide an overview of broad trends and identify an efficient, effective toolkit for growing and transforming your business profitability. Regardless of the challenges, I sincerely believe in God's love for us and that government and business, in cooperation with workers and consumers, can surmount the challenges we face if given clear leadership.

Acknowledgements

There are many to whom I am indebted for their examples, encouragement, or assistance in writing this book: Lesley Smith, Vice President of Logistics for Walmart Canada, for her inspiration, as watching her has shown me that the only ceiling we have to defeat is the one in our minds; Greg Shultiz, Vice President of Logistics, Walmart International, for reading and providing feedback on the title; Malcolm Gillihan, Vice President of Walmart US, for his living example of innovative Logistics and his high ethical standards; John Visser, Senior Director of Walmart International, for his support and advice; Olivier Joubert, Director of Logistics at Walmart Canada, for his consistent striving for excellence; Joe Plavetic, Odette Tadros, Mike Therrien and all the staff I worked with at Unilever for their support, encouragement and demonstration of how a matrix, profit-driven organization can be flexible and innovative; Jamie Fellowes of Fellowes for demonstrating what servant leadership and humility in a leader looks like; Peter Fellowes for his dedication to family and scholarship; Jim Edmonds for his example of what good accounting can accomplish; Doug Smith and the management board at Arla. In addition, I would like to thank Don Fiddes for his support over all the years. In addition to the many members of each team I have led, thank you for great work (you are too numerous to mention, but if it were not for you and your work and support, I could not have written this book). Having negotiated with hundreds of companies over the years, I would like to thank all the vendors for the lessons they taught me at the negotiating table and in operations on how business works. Traveling to countries from Israel, Italy, England, China, Hong Kong, and to the Philippines, has helped me see that while we are all different, our business goals can be aligned when based on profit. On the government side, departments in Canada, and US government programs have shown me that governments and government corporations want to succeed—they just need the same help businesses require. I would like to acknowledge all the women I have worked with who have taught me so much. There are too many to name, however a few deserve special mention: Lesley Smith, Odette Tadros, Samantha Plumstead, Virginia Garbutt, Connie Oliveria, Dorothy Hamilton, and Joanna Wardawa. I have learned a lot by watching you and working beside you.

Special thanks go to my wife Estela, for always supporting me through the long, seeming endless hours of writing and editing. Thanks also to our daughter Esther for being patient when I had to work on the book as she would much preferred to have been playing with me. Estela, Esther, and our daughter-to-be Ruth have all been an inspiration.

The ideas written here have been tried in different forms in business and tested in various situations and they provide Value Profit growth, I hope you enjoy them.

Chapter 1: Consumerism in Crisis

Over the next twenty years, we will experience dramatic changes in life style, consumption patterns and product design driven by the great recession, resource scarcity, climate change, the end of easy oil and water, food, and political crises. These issues seem far away until you realize that in cities and counties across North America, Europe, and Asia, the results of consumerism and unsustainable resource consumption are forcing leaders in governments and in Fortune companies to address the environmental consequences in ways that will affect us all. The oil spill in the Gulf of Mexico with the explosion and loss of the Deepwater Horizon is an example of the consequences of the choices we make to address fuel needs. Drill deep and risk disaster or allow prices to rise. There is no excuse for the environmental impact of the spill. However, BP and the other oil companies would not be drilling deep wells, spending billions to do so, if not for the demand consumers have placed on fuel sources. The most powerful, environmentally harmful addictions we face are our consumer energy and resource addictions. The cure for these addictions as a civilization if not managed properly will have an equally tremendous impact on employment and our living standards as the addictions themselves.

Last week as an example I was driving by a plastics bag plant, which opened six years ago to great fanfare with investments in machines and a new site. The owners had extensive plans for growth. The plans for a rail spur and silo development evaporated as companies shifted to a smaller bag size and bag imports from China increased. The next kicker they experienced was the focus on the impact of plastic bags on the environment. US plastic bag, sack, and wrap consumption ranges is over five hundred billion plastic bags annually, their impact on birds and pollution mobilized the environmental movement against bags. Although compared to paper, "plastic grocery bags consume 40 percent less energy, generate 80 percent less solid waste, produce 70 percent fewer atmospheric emissions, and release up to 94 percent fewer waterborne wastes."[4] However, reusable bags are a better environmental alternative, so a small tax on bags ensued in the city of the plastic bag plant. Net result—the once-new factory is closed and the building is for sale. This closure is an example of blowback from the feedback loop trying to correct environmental consequences of consumerism.

These corrections, while devastating for us in the short term will be, if not managed properly, even more devastating to our children.

Environmental agencies and corporations such as the Carbon War Room, Factor 4, Factor 10, Ceres, and USCAP are all working on plans to address carbon and water shortage. These plans will affect industries from fishing and food to paper box manufacturers, from electronics manufacturers to trucking companies to major global and small retailers. However, few companies have environmentally proofed their business to deal with the coming changes. An example is the shredder and offsite storage industries. Shredders and shredding services have traditionally been sold based on the fear of privacy violation. However, if I don't print it, I don't have to dispose of it. Our accountant recently wrote an article[5] on an ingenious way to efficiently scan paper and reduce waste. The day after the article came out, he had 119 requests for information. Many companies are going paperless, including Walmart. So, what does this mean for the shredding companies, offsite storage industry, and post offices in your country? It means a dramatic reduction in the need for shredders, shredding services, paper storage, and postal workers. Governments that are propping up such services need to develop legislative processes to address antiquated industries as the penetration of computers in North America and Europe means there are better cost-effective environmental alternatives. The question is what to do with workers whose jobs are eliminated.

Employment is one of the key questions we need to address when looking at the future. Changing to what Van Jones calls a Green Collar Economy[6] may be beneficial for companies, managers, and workers, but if governments and businesses transform themselves, without collaborating on employment policy, the economic impact will be disastrous. We need to face the trends now and withdraw investment from non-sustainable areas while reinvesting in the critical areas of innovative infrastructure and training. An example is computers and the automotive industry. Computers allow us flexibility to eliminate unnecessary resource consumption due to travel and can alter business models in many more ways than they have done. Automotive companies build and operate increasingly financially unsustainable companies, as shown by the billions required to keep them afloat. Governments continue to pour billions into industries that are not viable instead of cooperating to build a manufacturing base for integrated chips and monitors even though such high-tech manufacturing facilities will be critical in the future. If the world were an ice cream cone, humanity has eaten all the ice cream and only has the cone left to feed an increasing number of people. Therefore, we need to be selective on what pieces we give to whom. From a business perspective, this means we need to have a clear strategic vision for investment instead of investing in yesterday's technology. So, how did we get were we are?

Civilizations and Skewed Development?

Since 1492, when Christopher Columbus arrived in the Caribbean, the world has been experiencing skewed growth. Growth was skewed because the resources available to Western empires increased dramatically as Europeans exploited the massive resources of North and South

America. In addition, the Greco-Roman scientific and technical thought structure of Western Europe accelerated the population's advantage in warfare and physical goods production. Greek thinking concentrated on inquiries and debates into the nature of the world. Greeks strove to understand how and why the world operated with a concentration on the individual, which led the West to follow and appreciate science and technology. Plato, Aristotle, Pythagoras, Plotinus, and many more created thought paradigms that challenged and developed Western civilization's understanding of the physical world and options for governing. Jewish thinking reinforced these philosophical paradigms as Christianity spread throughout the West. The Christian empires of the West led the world in scientific exploration, building on the Greek model as they stove to understand more about who God is and how He revealed Himself in His creation.

Scientific investigation and prosperity exploded in Europe with the Renaissance and the Protestant Reformation. Scientists such as Isaac Newton, a staunch Christian, focused on scientific research to understand the truths about how God created the universe. Science was a political and military power multiplier for Western European empires as they leveraged the resources in the western hemisphere and their expanding scientific knowledge for expansion.

Islam also had exposure to Greco-Roman thinking and Jewish thought and from 1400 to 1500 experienced an explosion of science. Islamic military power at one point surpassed that of Western European empires,[7] however, this flowering of knowledge faded quickly amid internal strife. In 1492, the same year that Christopher Columbus came to the western hemisphere, the Moors were defeated in Spain. Islam was defeated from within as the Persians and the Ottoman Empire fought each other while eliminating their focus on scientific expansion.

Asian countries started from a different philosophical starting point to model the world.[8] Asians in the Chinese sphere of influence concentrated on harmony and the family. "Every Chinese was first and foremost a member of a collective or rather of several collectives-the clan, the village and especially the family."[9] Scientific knowledge was viewed as having limited utility, although the Chinese were incredible inventors, inventing gunpowder, clockwork, cast iron, the wheelbarrow, paper, pasta, ketchup, the printing press, and more. However, these ideas were never incorporated into a systematic, scientific method of study. Eastern philosophical models of Confucianism and Daoism and religions such as Buddhism did not have the same philosophical emphasis on exploring the universe. India also did not develop a scientific method, although they developed significant mathematical prowess with the invention of what we term today "Arabic" numbers.

Today, Western Europeans often think of their civilization as historically more creative and wealthier than Asian ones. However, this is a major historical error, as is the assumption that these countries were always poor and Western empires saved them from a horrible fate. In fact, for over three thousand years, China was the richest empire on the planet! This wealth facilitated a belief that the emperor was the Son of Heaven, sovereign over heaven, and that all foreign countries were vassals.[10] However, the invasions of the Mongols, along with China's internal struggles and lack of a scientific method, was to have an impact on their development. In 1570, Spain set out to colonize the Philippines, where the Chinese had long lived, resulting in approximately twenty thousand deaths.[11] Next, China had to deal with internal strife and a war with the Japanese over Korea in 1592. However, the seminal issue that still defines relations between China and Western countries today is the Opium Wars. European countries, America, and the British sold opium to Chinese in violation of morality and government policy. British forces, to support this trade and address what they saw as unjust Chinese practices, forced their way into China using the very weapons invented by the Chinese (gunpowder and cannons), but which had now been innovated with stronger metals. Gladstone, a British politician, declared, "A war more unjust in its origins, a war more calculated to cover this country with permanent disgrace, I do not know and have not read of." Western nations exploited China to such an extent that the

Chinese government's moral ability to govern failed. This has affected China's view of the West to this day.

While differences in philosophy, knowledge, and science had an impact, access to easily accessible coal and oil compounded Western growth. The application of low-cost energy has been a key mechanism since the industrial revolution for the expansion of empires and financial business models utilized by countries such as Holland, England, Germany, Britain, and the United States. Key Western civilization inventions such as the train, steel ships, electrical generation, and gas-powered cars and tanks and aircraft have all been based on using energy servants to project military force faster and more powerfully against opponents. The hydrogen bomb itself is an energy weapon, facilitated by our ability to project energy using jet engines.

In food production, the use of fuel to generate ammonia and nitrogen has also allowed energy to aide Western food development and export to other areas. This use of energy servants has dramatically increased the wealth and accompanying carbon footprint of European countries and members of the Organization for Economic Co-operation and Development, including Japan and Korea, over the last two hundred years.

In the late twentieth century, the global imbalance in knowledge, resources, and energy created from the fifteenth till the early twentieth century has been altered by US government polices that have shifted part of the core manufacturing base of US, Canada, and Europe to Japan, Korea, and then to China. An even more important transition has been the shift in the engineering and intellectual development of software products to India, China, Ireland, and the Philippines as those nations have increased their engineering ability based on Western exportation of technical information. The shift in manufacturing to Asia from the United States was initially the result of US government policies to develop Germany and Japan subsequent to World War II. In its fight with the Soviet Union, the United States also utilized the growth of economic relationships with politicians in countries susceptible to Communism to slow the spread of Communism and reduce exposure to the Marxist Communist model. Consumerism and major retail discount-chain growth, which required cheap products to flourish, also affected policy decisions to move production overseas.

In the last thirty years, manufacturers increasingly shifted production overseas to low-cost areas such Mexico, Honduras, Vietnam, Cambodia, and India to achieve even lower prices. However, the largest manufacturing plant in the world that generates TVs, plastic toys, braises, and cars is in China. Initially starting with Singapore, South Korea, and the other Asian Tigers, China in the late twentieth century became a powerhouse of manufacturing. Deng Xiaoping's Southern China tour prior to the Communist Party meeting in Beijing in 1992 had a dramatic impact on China accelerating economic changes that had started previously but which had slowed down with the impact of the Tiananmen Square massacre. The 1980s and 1990s were the start of Guangdong Province's prosperity. From 1985 to 1994, the province's exports increased from $2.9 billion to $50 billion.

Domestically, the Chinese people between 1980 and 1985 "bought more than 150 million bicycles, 250 million wristwatches, and 100 million (mostly black-and-white) television sets. From 1985 to 1990, China consumed another 120 million bicycles, 130 million electric fans, 50 million washing machines, 40 million refrigerators, and 120 million (increasingly color) television sets."[12] In one example, Frank Lo Kit-Lu, a Hong Kong businessman in the first year of production in China, noted, "2,000 workers made 14 million brassieres, more than 12 million of which were shipped to the United States. Under the so-called Multi-Fiber Agreement which governs the international trade in garments, Mr. Lo triggered the imposition of a United States quota for the importation of Chinese brassieres."[13] This explosion of exports from China was financed by billions of dollars from foreign, but mostly overseas Chinese and Japanese investors and by the use of a lot of inexpensive oil to allow for shipments across the Atlantic and Pacific oceans.

The people of China are the working resource that allows the country to manufacture items at a very low-rate wage, and the ocean container is the mechanism that allows the product to be moved at low cost. Chinese workers are usually very young migrant workers from the farming areas of China. China's population census figures show the number of migrant workers grew from 20 million in 1990 to 132 million in 2006.[14] A manager in China explained to me the internal travel restrictions and the challenges of getting a residency card in a different city. Often, she told me, people would marry someone from another city so they could get a residency card. Although a national ID card facilitates temporary residence in the cities, it is very difficult to get permanent residency, and if both parents are migrants, this affects their ability to get education for their child. However, the World Bank's brief on "Rural to Urban Migration in China," by Alan de Brauw and John Giles, shows that the average income of poor households rose as a result of migration. Although there was an accompanying negative effect on high school enrollment as migrants are usually employed in "occupations requiring no more than a junior high school education."[15] The average hourly compensation wage rate in China, based on an IMF report, was fifty-seven cents in 2002—forty-one cents in the country, and ninety-five cents in cities.[16] Although compensation has increased since 2002, it remains low due to the large unemployment rates in China, which are a danger to any Chinese government, as civil unrest is a major reason for Chinese governments' failures.

To address the need for growth internally, the Chinese government facilitates companies moving inland, which aides companies who can access labor at a reduced wage. While I was in China, a company I visited told me they were outsourcing their Chinese call center from Shenzhen to a city farther inland since they could get workers at a lower rate. This multi-billion-dollar corporation was willing to dislocate a trained organized center to gain a few more dollars of profit. This is one of the reasons I believe this book is critical for business as North American business leaders of many companies do not understand the impact low wages in countries outside of the United States and Europe are having, not only on workers in those countries but also on the consumers who are really workers in the West. Too often, we forget that to consume we need to work, and that outsourcing impacts wages in the West. To quote Robert Bruno, a professor at the University of Illinois, "What's happening is we are creating low-income workers who become low-wage consumers who seek low-priced goods."[17] To quote Danny Wegman, president of Wegman's grocery chain, from Ellen Shell's book, "Profit is critical. It's essential for everything we want to do, everything we can do. But for us it's a measure, not a goal. If we don't make a profit we feel we've done something wrong for our employees and, therefore, for our customers. We prefer to focus on our employees and let profit take care of itself."[18] Profit is critical, but employees/consumers should come first because it is workers who innovate and come up with ideas to transform the landscape of competition. Such ideas include the steel container, which has allowed the transition of industry to Asia.

The lowest of wages in Asia would not have allowed retail companies around the world to get cheap products due to the cost of shipping where it not for Malcolm McLean. In 1956, Malcolm McLean invented and patented the shipping container and subsequently started Sea-Land Shipping, as he wanted an easier way to move cargo. The US military standardized the containers in the 1970s, and the result was that while in 1956, loose cargo cost $5.86 per ton to load, utilizing an ISO shipping container, cost-reduced the cost to approximately $0.16 cents per ton. Malcolm Mc Lean changed the world and the lives of billions because of his invention[19]. The invention of the shipping container allowed logistics companies to move goods around the world at significantly lower costs, aided by ocean carriers such as Maersk, Hanging, NYK, and China Ocean Shipping Co (COSCO). The Asian trade alone utilizes thousands of ocean containers to move food and consumer products to global retail markets.

Retailing

The retail battlefield has forced manufacturers to supply products at ever-lower costs, irrespective of the actual value of the product. Manufacturers and farmers initially had market supremacy due to resource control and product and brand differentiation. These factors allowed manufacturers in the nineteenth and twentieth centuries to leverage their brands for higher profits. However, a shift in power to retailers started close to the end of the twentieth century with power shifting mainly to retailers from 1940 to 1980 following the change in US regulations governing pricing.

US retail innovation traces its origins back to John Wannamaker. Wannamaker, a haberdasher in 1875, bought an abandoned freight depot and turned it into what many regard as America's first grand department store. Wannamaker bought in bulk, invented the price tag, and created what was later called "the January White Sale."[20] Woolworth, S.S. Kiege Company, Sears, and others all jumped on the bandwagon of a cheap retailing market position. However, none of these men would have been able to accomplish this transition were it not for the fact that consumers shifted away from quality toward price. "America in the 1970's could not have been more receptive to the concept of swapping style, variety and durability for price."[21] The oil crisis in the seventies, inflation, and unemployment all drove a desire for lower costs. The opportunity to get products assumed to be of value at low prices helped shift the country from higher quality products to lower priced, lower quality goods, especially in clothing, and now in food and other products.

This low-price model is dependent on long supply chains but provides low price in the destination countries due to low wages at origin and the low cost of container shipping. However, it is fuel intensive. "Fuel costs represent as much as 50–60% of total ship operating costs, depending on the type of ship and service. Consider the following example. A large, modern container vessel used in the trans-Pacific trade has an actual maximum container capacity of 7,750 TEUs (twenty-foot equivalents) or 3,875 FEUs (forty-foot equivalents). With the cost of bunker fuel at $552 per ton and with fuel consumption at 217 tons per day, a single 28-day round trip voyage for this one vessel would produce a fuel bill of $3,353,952. This number could be greater for a number of reasons, such as if the voyage were more than 14 days, or if the vessel were smaller and less fuel efficient per container, or if schedule delays required the vessel to speed up to stay on schedule."[22]

Outsourcing manufacturing to Asia, which is dependent on high carbon fuel use, has led to increasing international trade deficits with Asian countries such as China and Japan. However, without quality improvements, this could not have happened to the extent it has. I distinctly remember my father, who ran an import-export business, showing me Japanese tools and products and telling me that the quality was poor. He then showed me products from Germany, the United States, and Europe and stressed their high quality. This was to change quickly over the next twenty years as the Japanese applied the principles of Deming, quality assurance and control, to their industries while developing their own technological focus with the process work done by Toyota on JIT and Lean Manufacturing and by Honda, Sony, and other companies. A brief history of trade with Asia shows the United States having its first deficit with Japan in 1965 as transistor radios and improving quality started a transformation.

In manufacturing and retail, the supply chain and systems area of the Value Chain have become critical differentiators. Efficient supply chains focused on continuous improvement aided Toyota, Unilever, Nestle, Walmart, Tesco, and Amazon toward growth and expansion. Ineffective supply chains with inefficient systems, material planning capability, and higher logistic cost models led companies such as Kmart in the United States, Eaton's in Canada, and many other retail businesses to file Chapter 11, declare bankruptcy, and close or reduce operations. However, retail pressure for lower prices has increased as supply chain cost reductions narrow. Manufacturers have fought back with mergers and acquisitions. However, with the shift to lower-quality products and mass retailing, very few manufacturers, with the exception of companies such as Unilever, Proctor and Gamble, and Nestlé's, with their extensive portfolio of products, brand-equity companies such as Coke and Pepsi, and innovative companies like GE and Apple, have maintained their strength in the market. Even these companies face increasing pressure to provide cheaper and cheaper products, resulting in less employment, differentiation, and larger, massive production lines.

However, based on the Great Recession and the economic and environmental challenges we face, retailers, manufacturers, and governments need to review the concept that cheap products are beneficial. This desire for cheap products, while aiding many developing countries to get kick started, has hollowed out American manufacturing and created a problem in global trade and risk management. The existing economic model, as was shown from 2007 to 2009, is unsustainable. While many blame the Great Recession on the sub-prime mortgage situation, the reality is that consumers and companies, especially in the United States and Europe, have allowed trade surpluses with China to continue until China has achieved $2 trillion in cash reserves. Japan, Germany, and some other countries have also grown their trade surpluses at the expensive of the United States, the United Kingdom, and Australia, among others. In 2008–2009, consumers in the United States, Canada, and Europe were impacted economically, reducing overseas buying by 20 percent, which resulted in thousands of factory closures in China. This drop in volume, along with higher fuel costs, affected shipping companies, who therefore lost billions. "At current prices, we aren't making money on any route," said Ulrich Kranich, executive board member in charge of global operations, summing up the main reason for Hapag-Lloyd's financial woes.[23] No major shipping companies were profitable in 2009. Most steamship lines, except for Maersk and a few others, survived due to the support of their governments. To address this, ocean carriers removed large numbers of ships from their fleets to reduce capacity and costs. Retailers faced a dramatic decline in capacity, affecting their ability to move freight to meet advertising deadlines and seasonal merchandise changes. Steamship profits must increase for carriers to put back into service vessels they removed to reduce capacity and create price increases. Ocean transportation costs have now become part of ground zero in the battle for price, and this will continue for some time given the inordinate amount of fuel it takes to move products across long supply chains. While maritime capacity has increased since the economic slump, capacity is still not back to the levels of pre-slump as ships have been removed from service, slow steaming has been implemented and the larger new vessels have not off set this as demand has again risen for goods from China. In addition slow steaming and the lack of orders for containers from steamship lines in the prior year caused a container shortage as China volumes surged. Prices therefore remain high. What does this mean for road and rail carriers, which increasingly face freight reduction demands from shippers? It means land transportation will be the next battleground for price increases as domestic goods shipments decrease, and increasingly shipments are from port to distribution center (DC), to store reducing backhaul opportunities. This will be the next battle as retailers and manufacturers try to control their transportation to reduce costs; this is where small companies will face off against major, billion-dollar players, and where transport companies will increasingly lose, as they do not have the power of the billion-dollar manufacturers. Even DHL, Canadian National, and Canadian Pacific companies supported by their governments will be forced to reduce costs as road carriers are increasingly forced to accept 2–4 percent net profit—a profit close to the range many retailers and manufacturers will find it beneficial to pay as they have to fight off higher ocean rates and consumer credit concerns. In such a market, it is better to invest in stocks than in the infrastructure required to run a transportation fleet unless you have a cost-plus arrangement. This will further drive down consumer/worker wages and end with the elimination of many middle-class management roles that transportation and warehousing businesses in North America support.

In the battlefield of retailing so far, you can see that US companies are ahead of Europe and now lead the world in retailing based on the annual figures below.

Walmart	$404B
Carrefour	$124B
Metro AG	$95.78B
Tesco	$93.85B
Kroger	$75.35B
Costco	$71.42B
Home Depot	$67.6B
Aldi	$65.7B
Target	$64.74B
Walgreens	$63.34B

Presently, there are no Chinese, Indian, or Brazilian companies on that list. If Robert Fogel's forecast is correct and China becomes a $123 trillion-dollar economy in 2040 with a per capita income of UF$85,000, this will change. Even the Carnegie Endowment for International Peace predicts China's economy will be 20 percent larger than the United States' by 2050.[24] The Chinese, having used the leverage provided by low wages and damaging their environment, need now to grow their retail presence if they want to become the largest economy in the world with 40 percent of global GDP.[25] This will dramatically affect globalization and the Value Chain equation. While there are risks to China's growth due to politics and its banking system, we need to think strategically about the relationship we have with the Chinese globally, given our dependencies. The GDP of Europe, the United States, and Canada has gone from 68 percent of global GDP in 1950 to 47 percent in 2007,[26] and it will continue to fall. As fertility rates drop and the population ages in Europe, North America, and Japan, the tremendous economic growth engine that Western countries have been for the world will slow. Unless we plan for it as China is doing with Brazil by developing an economic relationship, our relationships will not be where they need to be with the new people, new corporations, and new economic powers of the future, such as China, India, and Brazil.

If Western consumers continue to demand cheap Asian products via retail channels, trading jobs that make things for jobs as servants of others, destroying the environment, and shifting power to Asia, the West will become significantly less important and employment will continue to fall. So what is the alternative? *Is* there an alternative to the opium of cheap products and environmental destruction? The good news is there is an alternative in value and innovation.

Chapter 2: Our Value

One major root cause of our global issues is how we value people, land, products, and resources. More importantly, how do we value ourselves? Slavery is illegal, though an international standard for the worth of human life has been created that is opposed to the belief that a person's life is above value. Internationally, the value for a quality year of life is $50,000 for insurance purposes. However, "Stanford economists have demonstrated that the average value of a year of quality human life is actually closer to about $129,000."[27] This number was arrived at as the US government debated using cost-benefit analysis to decide whether medical treatment should take place. Many countries do similar analyses; in the United States, as the article referenced mentions, the US government has established a soldier's life as worth US$500,000. However, this is undervaluing a soldier, as the Environmental Protection Agency office estimates the value of of a person's life is now $7.22 million.[28]

Raj Patel addresses such valuations using Joseph Stiglitz's work in this area and traces this change to the Speenhamlamland laws in England in the eighteenth century, which elites used at the time to change society.[29] Patel traces the connection between Nazi economists Karl Binding and Alfred Hoche's book, *Permission for the Destruction of Life Unworthy of Life*,[30] where they argued for killing those they deemed unworthy of life, and present-day decision-making processes which utilize the very processes initially decreed by the United States and others. I thought such comments might be overblown until I read a recent article in the *Economist*, which had these words in reference to environmental conservation: "the nasty truth is that the likelihood of random and violent death may be the cheapest form of conservation yet invented."[31] If this comment in a globally recognized magazine does not scare you into remembering the Nazis and their valuation of human life, read Steve Milloy's book, *Green Hell*.[32] While I do not agree with Milloy's apparent opposition to action to address environmental issues, I agree with his opposition to the extremism that many justify in the name of saving the planet. What we need is innovation and transformational changes, not extremism. It is important that ethical businesspeople become involved and engaged in addressing the issues we face. If we do not, in twenty to thirty years it will be our aging lives that are calculated into the price equation, and at that point, we will have few options remaining.

In the same way we are undervaluing our lives, we have undervalued lives in China, India, and the East, which strive to satisfy our desire for products and services. The life of a man, woman, or child in the East is worth much less than that of a person in the West. This is a dangerous precedent because once the tables turn, as they will by 2040 with China, we will be paying the price of this blowback.[33]

Western civilization presently utilizes a distribution model where value is established at the end of a supply chain, not at the beginning. This establishment of value at the end of the supply chain undervalues the resources, labor, and intelligence incorporated into the product at origin. This is partially the responsibility of economics and politics as China undervalues the Yuan to provide employment and aid China's need for investment. It is also a consequence of globalization, which correctly encourages the movement of production to the lowest-cost environment. However, this movement of production to the lowest-cost environment should only be done after factoring in the impact on nature and people involved in the production. At the same time, the creation of value at destination is a challenge for corporations because the consumer does not understand the production inputs and corporations' struggles with pricing policies, as they presently do not have a mechanism to price the true value into the product. By true value, I am referring to the value of all inputs (labor, water, fuel, destruction of habitats to get minerals, and loss of animals and plants that we need for oxygen) and the value in the customers' minds based on the resources available. Below is a chart showing normal inputs into a pricing model for a product and the cost elements that are missing today. The innovation or customer-perceived value is the delta which allows for greater profit margins. Establishing value in this way only works efficiently on a global basis to manage resources and government policy if you factor in the missing cost elements.

Establishment of Value

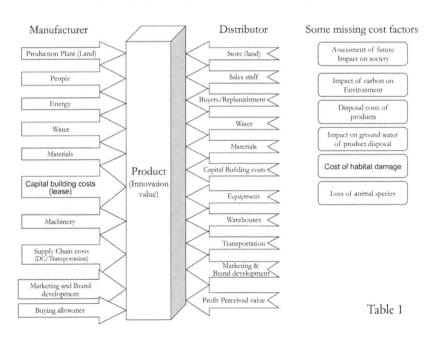

Table 1

In the view of Paul Hawken and the Lovins, our existing models have not included the natural capital embedded in the product, which is the cost of all natural inputs.[34]

Take a Bratz doll, which is type of doll like a Barbie doll. Four of these dolls sell for less than US$10 in some retail stores. Yet, each of these dolls' plastic components, once molded, is hand crafted. A person installs the hair with a high-powered sewing machine, and then each has a personal hairdresser in a factory who combs and grooms the hair with gel and gives it a hairstyle. Another person applies makeup, and others dress the doll. The price of these dolls is undervalued since labor in China is priced cheaply. However, if the price was closer to the true value, it would include the missing factors, and many fewer dolls would be manufactured, sold, and dumped. Since children will still require such toys, demand will exist for a higher-quality, longer-lived item and a smaller, less resource-intensive, lower-priced item. The higher-priced doll could be resold or recycled, and the lower-priced item could be recycled. However, this does not occur, as we now have the ability to price everything but have no concept of the true value of anything and are incapable in many cases of establishing the appropriate cost and price. I have seen poor families spend money on toys they will soon dump and very little on products that will grow their children's abilities. This is not just poor families. We know families where the children attend grade schools with blended classes. Their kids receive low marks and complain of the education while the parents continue to send them there when they can afford much better. Again, how we value a service, education in this case, is the problem.

Modern civilization has reached a plateau of development and expansion based on present financial and business models. Universities and colleges are training students in specialties for which there are limited jobs, as the jobs have moved overseas. Major programming centers are now located in Ireland, the Philippines, and India, where companies like Infosys can hire excellent talent at low rates, or overseas staff have been contracted to work in Europe or the United States. The point is not that work has been outsourced but that the total global aggregate demand for workers is not high enough to utilize all the available talent. To use the human intellectual creative resources we have as a global civilization requires more innovations to drive sustainability and employment, not less. Unfortunately, innovations are limited as business capital is continuously allocated to low-priced, mass-produced, homogeneous items, just as the Jones' products are the trend due to the high costs of trial and invention. In addition, many companies have no method or knowledge of how to make innovation visible for investment or how to judge its viability. This is a critical issue for European and North American populations since they no longer manufacture many items and must rely on innovation to drive growth and development. The good news is that some Western companies are still building better mousetraps, such as Apple with the iPod. However, such innovations are limited and when successful need to include the full product cost, including recycling and disposal.

As we approach 2030, we need to understand the value we place on life versus the value we place on having lower-cost products. We are a capitalist society, and value and price drive our decisions. Increasingly, global manufacturing and supply chains will be challenged as customers experience the consequences of business and consumer decisions to opt for cheap short-term solutions versus longer-lasting sustainable ones. You can read many books on the topic of the global challenges we are facing, many describing drastic changes. Some of the recent ones are:

> *Keeping Our Cool* by Andrew Weaver a lead author for three IPCC reports on Climate change. This book takes you through climate change science and identifies challenges we face.

> *Climate Wars* by Gwynne Dyer, which takes you through alternative futures, escalating the degree of impact climate change will have on the world's political stability.

> *Global Warring* by Ceo Paskal also addresses the question on how environmental, economic, and political crises will affect the world.

What Next? by Chris Pattern is an excellent read, as his political understanding as a former British MP, the last governor of Hong Kong, and chancellor of Oxford shows.

Peak Everything wake up to a century of declines by Richard Heinberg addresses the declines we face due to oil, fresh water and climate.

Balancing out the climate extreme position is the perspective provided by scientists who take a different position on how the issue of climate change and how quickly we need to changes such as:

Climate of Extremes by Patrick J. Michaels and Robert C. Balling Jr. takes a position on climate change and reviews the science from the perspective that there are concerns with the models used and that extremism will be very damaging.

The Deniers by Lawrence Solomon reviews the issues some renown scientists have with extreme climate change science.

Alternative future projections from writers on the extreme and moderate sides of climate change show us we need to make well planned and thought out changes. These adjustments in behavior and product design will all affect what, where, and when we buy. The battlefield of retailing is where these changes will take play out. In the book, *Retailing Marketing*,[35] Malcolm Sullivan and Dennis Adcock describe the fourfold impact retailing has on an area:

- ✓ First is the physical role in respect to its site. For instance, is the development in a derelict area or greenfield?

- ✓ Second is the economic effect that retail has on a locality, both as an employer and generator of table income.

✓ Third is the fact that it becomes a focus for consumer spending in the area.

✓ Fourth, they identify the social role that shopping and shop visiting have, which affect local interactions.

To these four, however, we need to add the following:

✓ Fifth, the sustainable footprint of the store and retail chain.

✓ Sixth, the environmental impact a brand position and its strategic sourcing strategy have on the origin and destination countries and peoples.

✓ Seventh, the natural capital impact a company has on the society and culture in which it operates.

As a businessperson, you are probably applying a number of tools to validate your product offering, such as the Cooper Stage Gate product development process, hiring superstar companies like IDEO to drive product ideas, or utilizing market research from processes such as discourse analysis, semiotics, ethnographics, and need-states analysis.

However, such tools can only provide an indication as to your product's future success. What customers want is always the question. Recently, I was speaking with the CMO for a shoe company, and he mentioned that a key difference between Europeans and Americans was North Americans see products as disposable while most Europeans do not. This is a key point because a disposable society is not a sustainable society, and a sustainable society is a different business model, requiring a different financial and value chain paradigm.

Take shoes, for example. I can buy a pair at my local shoe store for $50 to $99 dollars, and it may last six months to two years. Over nine years, I will spend approximately $900 replacing the original pair based on today's pricing, excluding the environmental impact, which, at a minimum, will be twice the value, so let's say $1800 dollars. Alternatively, I could spend $285 and buy a pair of Allen Edmonds. Ninety-six percent of those shoes are "Made in America," and will last me at least nine years with three re-craftings for a cost of $582. Given the product is leather, the disposal impact is less, so I estimate the total including disposal at $782. So, which is the better value for the money? While the disposal costs are only estimates, the answer in my opinion, are the Allen Edmonds, which will last longer and look better for years with the proper care. Since I have not visited their factory, I cannot do a complete assessment on the environmental impact of their production plant. However, in speaking with them I learned they use calf leather purchased in Chicago, with some from Italy so their products will look better (much better than $99 shoes, I suspect!) and last longer. There are, I am sure, processes they could change to be more sustainable, such as reducing corrugate usage, which they have tried. However, given these shoes are made in the United States, the social, employment and carbon footprint benefit is significant compared to products shipped from overseas.

Shoes are a good example of the choices we face as business leaders relative to the everyday products we buy and sell. Do we continue to develop products that have limited life and undervalue human life, or do we build better-quality products that will be durable and last longer? This question is critical as we decide on marketing strategies that will shape our nation's desires for either cheap, low–profit, non-sustainable products or longer-lasting, durable, recyclable, value-added products. Major retailers have tried to develop brand positions based on sustainability. However, the challenge is their brand-value messages do not match corporate strategies of low cost, which drive a large environmental footprint, unneeded and unnecessary consumption, and low wages. To address this, we need retailers and manufacturers to adopt new corporate models and marketing plans—models and plans driven by sustainability and real measures of environmental value, not ones where quality standards have been lowered to meet low-priced needs. Low value, low quality, non-recyclable products will cost us the environment, our living standard, and our business. Key to accomplishing change is economic modeling. Some modern economic models including one by Robert Costanza and the one proposed by Paul Hawken and the Lovins of the Rocky Mountain Institute in their book Natural Capitalism include natural capital into the forms of capital we value. Their definition of natural capital goes beyond that of the World Bank, which defines natural capital as resources. The four forms of capital identified by Hawkens and the Lovins are:[36]

- ✓ Human capital, in terms of labor intelligence, culture, and organization;

- ✓ Financial capital—cash, investments, and monetary instruments;

- ✓ Manufactured capital, including infrastructure, tools, and factories;

- ✓ Natural capital, made up of resources, living systems, and ecosystem services.

Incorporating natural capital into financial calculations provides a more realistic pricing of the cost and value of production and growth. We define existing profit calculations that do not include natural capital as Easy Profits and calculations that include natural capital as Value Profits.

- ✓ Easy Profit is defined as profit excluding natural capital costs versus

- ✓ Value Profit, which is defined as profit after incorporating natural capital costs.

If we focus only on Easy Profits we leave ourselves open to disaster and business collapse. Business collapse which as we have experienced is a dark, horrible network virus, so as business leaders and planners, we need to develop an antiviral. In 2000, we developed a business plan to address Y2K. If you were in business then, you were probably perched on the edge of your seat, waiting on the call that would tell you if the business world was about to collapse. You know what, it never did! Basically, nothing happened, although as a world we spent billions and billions of dollars on consultants, new systems, and business plans. The reality was it was a non-event as people, businesses, and governments spent so much time doing advance work to stop the problem. Some might say that the issue was overblown, but I would say better prepared than an economic disaster. Business collapse, as we saw with the global automotive, financial, and housing networks, is not a joke! In 1999, while working at Unilever, we spent days and weeks preparing. We had global conferences and global conference calls. We had weekly, almost daily planning sessions, we purchased new computers, replaced ERP systems, and ensured our partners in all industries were prepared with fixes in place. Y2K was not a disaster but only because of the work that people, businesses, and governments did.

In the same way, H1N1 was not the disaster predicted due to preparation. H1N1 was the second time we developed a global plan to prevent disaster, and it worked. There is a verse in the Bible, Proverbs 29:18, that says, "Where there is no vision the people perish."[37] In life and in business, we need vision to see what is coming. In *The Innovators Dilemma*, Clayton M. Christensen discusses how industries are blindsided by disruptive innovations because they focus on specific areas to the neglect of others. In the same way, we can focus on just selling products, or we can prepare for the disruptions that will be coming while also aiming for growth. If we prepare, we will be ready to face the future disruptions better armed and more profitable than if we do not. Even better, if we prepare as a network of businesses locally and globally, we can avert disaster as we did with Y2K and H1N1. Today, with God's help, we can avert disaster if we learn from Y2K, H1N1, and the Great Recession, a case where we failed to address the issues.

Chapter 3: Broad-Based Disruptions

In 2009, we had the worst economic crisis the world had seen since the Great Depression. An estimated five to eighteen trillion dollars[38] were ripped from future support for Health Care, payment of debt, and the tax-paying population to pay for the bad judgment of central and public banks, governments, and a few large business leaders. The Great Recession ripped the guts and heart out of the US and global economy, pushing us back into the economic past. The economic crisis devastated the economy at a level surpassing 9/11, Enron, and the Ecom collapse. US unemployment levels reached as high as 10 percent, and shipments from China to the world were down 20 percent. Employment in the world was devastated although Asia, India, and Brazil (which had changed its focus from the United States to China) quickly recovered some of their lost ground. In 2010, the crisis almost restarted in Europe with the debt burdens of Greece and other Europe counties, which required a $1-trillion (U.S.) economic rescue plan. Below you can see the US unemployment levels for the last ten years[39] and the UK rate, published by the UK Office for National Statistics on 20 January 2010 at 9:30 am.

TABLE 2	Labor Force Statistics from the Current Population Survey											
Labor force status: Unemployment rate					Age:	16 years and over				US Bureau of Labour Statistics		
Year	Jan	Feb	Mar	Apr	May	Jun	Jul	Aug	Sep	Oct	Nov	Dec
2000	4	4.1	4	3.8	4	4	4	4.1	3.9	3.9	3.9	3.9
2001	4.2	4.2	4.3	4.4	4.3	4.5	4.6	4.9	5	5.3	5.5	5.7
2002	5.7	5.7	5.7	5.9	5.8	5.8	5.8	5.7	5.7	5.7	5.9	6
2003	5.8	5.9	5.9	6	6.1	6.3	6.2	6.1	6.1	6	5.8	5.7
2004	5.7	5.6	5.8	5.6	5.6	5.6	5.5	5.4	5.4	5.5	5.4	5.4
2005	5.3	5.4	5.2	5.2	5.1	5	5	4.9	5	5	5	4.9
2006	4.7	4.8	4.7	4.7	4.6	4.6	4.7	4.7	4.5	4.4	4.5	4.4
2007	4.6	4.5	4.4	4.5	4.4	4.6	4.6	4.6	4.7	4.7	4.7	5
2008	5	4.8	5.1	5	5.4	5.5	5.8	6.1	6.2	6.6	6.9	7.4
2009	7.7	8.2	8.6	8.9	9.4	9.5	9.4	9.7	9.8	10.1	10	10
2010	9.7	9.7	9.7									

Table 3

UK Employment
Employment rate falls to 72.4 per cent

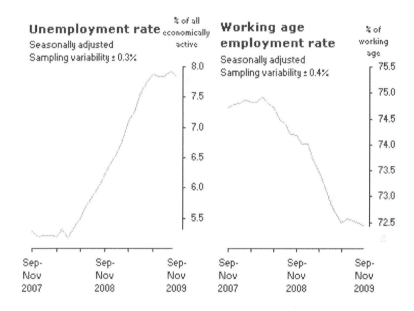

These rates, while high, do not show the impact on people who took part-time or lower-paying jobs or who dropped completely out of the job market. The Great Recession changed the way people look at the world and transformed the relationship between the developed and developing world and between businesses and workers. Parents come home and talk about layoff and loss of respect. The average duration of unemployment in the United States surpassed six months, a first since 1948, and for every open job in the United States, six people are actively looking for work.[41] There is unemployment, as Don Peck points out in an article in the *Atlantic*, and then there is chronic unemployment[42]. While unemployment has come down slightly from 10 percent in the United States, it will take years to come fully back if the way smaller recessions have played out occur. While this recession has been good for women in one sense, it has been devastating for families which require two incomes and where the man is unemployed. Additionally, since women have had a lower pay scale than men, even employment benefiting women has had a lower benefit on the family.

Coming out of this recession will be a challenge because resources have been committed to keeping old, industry-paradigm companies such as Chrysler, which has been in and out of bankruptcy so many times it could be a jack-in-the-box, afloat. As well, the economic environment will be required to face sustainable challenges it has never seen before.

The G7 still exists, but now the focus is on the G20, and the dollar has limited stability. We have the first Afro-American Democratic President in the White House, and he, like his predecessor, will struggle to fix the issues the peoples of the United States, Britain, and Europe helped create. Only due to the combined efforts of the top economies and developing economies such as India, China, and Russia were we able to step back from the edge of a Great Depression! We could detail all the things that went bad—General Motors, Ford, Chrysler, 2008's oil shock, the sub-prime mortgage debacle in the United States. The key thing to learn from the examples we just went over is that all these failures were not just one failure. It was not just one company that almost collapsed or just one industry. You need to acknowledge and understand that these failures were failures in structural business (banking) and governmental decision networks. Banks and governments are made up of people. These failures were a failure of all the people networks who bought into the idea of a better life built on credit and debt!

Spend now, buy cheap, and save later. The majority of us have accepted and bought into that advertising message, and now we are reaping the result. Nevertheless, as the decision networks are still lead by people with that same mindset, we face dangerous decisions. We face a time were as private individuals and business leaders we need to choose between spending now and using up all we have or planning for the future and building successful businesses and a successful world. We face choices in a time where the decisions we make *as business leaders and as people are critical for our present and our future.* Networked decision can be beneficial, and they can be dangerous. Think about the auto industry. It was not just one company (one node) of the automotive network that was in failure mode. It was General Motors and their network (Opel, Saab), Chrysler and its network, and even Ford came close.

These companies were led into failure due to poor decisions related to the market. They knew people do not buy SUVs when oil prices go up dramatically. Yet they wanted to maximize Easy Profits now and so continued to invest in SUVs that people would not buy if oil prices increased. They invested in vehicles that increased pollution and used up easily accessible oil at a fast rate. They continued to make large, non-sustainable vehicles when the demand and conditions were changing. The automotive leadership decisions affected not just the auto companies' divisions but also suppliers and the resource companies providing the raw materials. Magna was hit, and many auto suppliers and the steel, plastics, and cloth industries were affected. Trucking companies and railways were also hit, as were and everyone who was connected.

You were affected when the building industry slumped due to a lack of demand as consumers realized that the economy was not sustainable and as credit dried up. The auto companies struggled, and then GM and Chrysler went into bankruptcy. At the same time, oil prices dropped as decisions were made that the price was not sustainable in an economy which was about to collapse. I realize these are simplified explanations, but sometimes simple is best. I knew a vice president who worked in the sub-prime area, and he told me almost two years before the economic crisis that the market was not sustainable. People in the banks could see this coming but at the same time wanted to continue making money.

In the end, the banking sub-prime industry collapsed, but not before affecting a lot of people.

In the case of Enron, sub-prime mortgage, and the auto industry, people knew what was coming, but few did anything until we were in crisis. In the case of the few companies that made the right choices, they made billions. But why did we wait this long before making decisions? The reason, I think, is a network mentality that rewards conformity, lethargy, and a human desire not to change what has worked in the past and is easy.

In business, we suffer from a network mentality that rejects first movers and explorers. In *Connected*,[43] the authors make the point that we are all connected and discuss the theories of Six Degrees of Separation and Three Degrees of Influence. The point is that we are connected, we operate as people in networks, and so do our computers and businesses. Your business survives based on the relationships created with other companies and the people you service. Your business wins or dies based on your relationships with those buying your products and your suppliers. While we try to create firewalls via sourcing and purchasing rules, in the end the people contact is still the most critical thing you can do to get your business to succeed. People connections impact the way our businesses are connected internally via politics and the way the economy is connected, again via politics. If you are in business today, you are probably on LinkedIn. LinkedIn is like a business version of Facebook or Twitter, allowing you to stay connected to people in the business world. You access and see details about the people you have met or will be meeting. It is a great tool to enable you to get to know people before you meet them. Even those who do not like it still go on LinkedIn and maintain a profile or search for people. You can select who you are connected to—you have a choice, an option to see who wants to connect to you and to choose to connect to them. However, your sales staff have no choice. They need to stay connected to grow your business. LinkedIn is a great tool as it reduces the dangers of being a first mover in a relationship. You can get to know people, and it is easier to connect with them once you know their history. In the case of the depression that almost was, the very connectedness of the businesses resulted in failure. Just as in a computer, a system connection can be a strength, but it can also be a weakness if you get a virus.

The failure of these companies spread as their networks of purchasers aged, the message of their poor quality spread, and their product mix was not adjusted to meet the needs of the next disruption. When fuel prices spiked amid a customer credit crunch, they could not last. In today's global networked environment, we are all an email away from a problem and an opportunity—an opportunity to be socially, ethically, and morally responsible while positioning our companies and ourselves for the future.

The decision network in the companies mentioned failed to look at the future and make profitable decisions for Continual sustained growth. Don't make that mistake! The word "continual" is used here because sustainable businesses require continuous growth, so we need to acknowledge that upfront and aim for it while acknowledging that businesses have to address and incorporate the full cost of any business innovation. Continual sustained growth relates to why we work. Businesspeople believe in business and are committed to it as an inheritance or as a labor of love for their families to enjoy the nice things of life such as cottages, houses, vacations, and a good standard of living. Each person, each family leader, is driven to make things better for their family or themselves. Many like the challenges of business and growth and want to see what they have created for their families continue on. None of these people want to see their companies fail. Today, some people believe that businesses do not have the sophistication to understand that consumer choices and business decisions to satisfy those choices can destroy the very customers to whom they sell. And, in fact, many businesses do not have that understanding and give lip service to it, selling products that are environmentally unsustainable. An example is manufacturers and retailers who sell bottled water in countries where the water is very pure, when doing so uses up resources and affects our biodiversity. The "Living Planet 2008" report showed that "biodiversity, as measured by populations of 1,686 vertebrate species across all regions of the world, has declined by nearly 30 per cent over just the past 35 years (Figure 1)."[44]

The reality is most companies have plans, but only truly forward-thinking companies in the West plan beyond the next two years. The majority of businesses focus on making money in the short term. However, devastation results from such poor strategic vision around the environment. In the chart,[45] you can see the population densities for selected countries, and as you compare Monaco to China, you can see the difference in population densities between China and Denmark.

TABLE 4		Land Area	Pop. Density	Land Area	Pop. Density
COUNTRY	Population	(Sq Kms)	(Sq Kms)	(Sq Miles)	(Sq Miles)
Monaco	32,410	2	16,205	1	41971
Singapore	4,425,700	693	6,386	268	16540
Bahrain	688,300	665	1,035	257	2681
Bangladesh	144,319,600	144,000	1,002	55599	2596
Korea (South)	48,422,600	98,480	492	38023	1273
Philippines	87,857,500	300,000	293	115831	758
Japan	127,417,200	377,835	337	145883	873
India	1,080,264,400	3,287,590	329	1269345	851
Philippines	87,857,500	300,000	293	115831	758
UK	60,441,500	244,820	247	94525	639
Germany	82,431,400	357,021	231	137847	598
Italy	58,103,000	301,230	193	116306	500
Switzerland	7,489,400	41,290	181	15942	470
China	1,306,313,800	9,596,960	136	3705405	353
Denmark	5,432,300	43,094	126	16639	326
France	60,656,200	547,030	111	211209	287
Mexico	106,202,900	1,972,550	54	761606	139
UAE	2,563,200	82,880	31	32000	80
USA	295,734,100	9,629,091	31	3717811	80
Canada	32,805,000	9,976,140	3	3851808	9

The densities of China and Denmark are very similar, and yet China has some of the worst pollution, with two of the top ten most polluted cities in the world.[46] China, India and Russia, each have two cities on the top ten list. In the case of China this relates specifically to the development focus it has taken to lift the country out of poverty, reduce unemployment, and stabilize the country by focusing on increasing its manufacturing base with low-end manufacturing jobs and minimal expenditures for pollution control. This is a clear business choice. In the same way, the United States' commitment to monoculture farming and water use is creating a water crisis.

The most strategic business plans recognize environmental impact years in advance. One illustration is at one company (let's call them A) who assessed commercial fisheries and identified that the fish supply was in danger. They also identified that North Americans and many Europeans like fish with little taste, and that the remaining stocks had a stronger flavor. A therefore made a decision to sell their fish consumer-packaging businesses well in advance of the failure of ocean fishing based on their own analysis, which showed global fisheries were overextended and would require reductions in fishing to survive. This was advanced, long-term planning at work. In 2006, two to three years after they made their decision and while they were still exiting the fisheries business, it was reported: "Boris Worm and colleagues shocked the world by declaring overfishing would put every single commercial fishery in the world out of business before 2050 and the oceans might never recover based on their four-year scientific investigation, the most extensive ever done."[47] Company A had recognized a challenge and dealt with it in advance. The question you need to ask yourself is what company would buy into a failing industry?

The answer is many mid-to-small companies do, as their business often cannot afford talented expert researchers and analysts. The second question you need to ask yourself is why A did not stop fishing and shift their business model to focus on stewardship of a limited resource. Stewardship of resources is critical to economic stability, business planning, and sustainability. The answer is that A was utilizing natural capital at no cost to itself, as were the other fleets, and since A could not by itself control global fisheries and there is no overall control, stewardship was not a business option. So, by selling the business A made a strategic business move and dumped a risk. Unfortunately, company B, the company they sold to, now has to over fish a failing fish stock to achieve the profitability targets required for the debts they assumed. A solution to this problem would be a global fisheries management program. It would be a program under which companies A and B and industry partners agreed to licenses and quota for fleets. Then, when a sale is required and a company like A wants to limit its risk, they can do so by creating a joint stewardship program where A would contribute to developing an alternative model with B so both could benefit. Instead, today's fleets move to countries and areas where over fishing is still possible.

The alternatives of programs like a global fisheries management or government and business alliances for strategic stewardship are seldom used or effective because companies without legislation, and sometimes even with legislation, focus on Win-Win-Lose strategies as opposed to Win-Win-Win strategies. A Win-Win-Win strategy is where:

> First Win: both companies win.

> Second Win: environmental stewardship is a given.

> Third Win: the general population's health and benefit is maximized at both origin and destination—from where the products are reaped from the lands or sea to where they are finally consumed.

It is usually when business utilize dysfunctional solutions to problems focusing on the normal negotiating paradigms of Win-Lose or Win-Win to make money that problems are created, not the desire to make money and have a continuous cash flow. Many quote Jesus incorrectly when they say money is the root of all evil. In fact, Jesus said that the "love of money is the root of all evil." No one wants to be poor, and no company wants to be known for doing wrong. They know what a poor reputation could mean to their brand, so they plan for the future.

I have worked for the world's largest retailer, one of the top three food companies in the world, and private industry, traveling to countries from Europe to Asia. I have presented to boards, participated in global strategic marketing planning sessions, and seen corruption firsthand when people decide that they will take advantage of their positions. All businesspeople make choices about money—how to make it, how to spend it, and what to do with it. However, we need to sit down and weigh the impact of those decisions. Will my company make money for one year, for five years, and then have a problem versus having a regular growing revenue stream for ten to twenty years? If I take the same attitude as Adam Smith, my motivation will not be just about immediate profits but about maximizing profit and shareholder and social value for as long as possible. My profit interests must align with the long-term needs of the consumers and society I live in.

During the early nineties, I worked in the auto industry in Quality Assurance and attended a conference where one of the leading Japanese professors was to speak to automotive leaders on quality assurance. This man was very famous, and automotive companies flew in vice presidents and directors for the event. I was pleased to be able to attend for my company.

Now, at this time we knew Japanese cars were much better quality and we knew we had to change, but no one wanted to make the commitment. So in walks this quality leader. He lectures us for two or three hours on quality in Japanese (it was translated into English) and the gist of the message was that North American leaders were idiots who knew they were making bad-quality products and yet continued to do so. This professor basically called every Canadian and American in the room an idiot. At the end of the speech, everyone aside from me stood up and applauded the message, but nothing really changed. Shortly thereafter, I left the automotive industry. Now, why am I telling you this story? The reason is the global business environment is similar. We have many people telling us we have a problem, but few are trying to deal with issues. We are like the blind men who met an elephant. Each touches a section of the elephant, but they cannot together see the big picture. The reason many large companies see sustainability as a positive is they see the dollars in it. Environmental stewardship can be profitable for all companies, since if you consume less, your costs reduce. This works in times such as we face now, where businesses and consumers have less appetite for risk due to less credit, social unrest, and consumers spending less. However, if we focus only on spending less, we will miss the boat to the future.

You still need to sell services and products. Let's call our product a Twig. You need to sell this Twig, and you operate in a business environment for which you have made assumptions and built your business, your network for success. If you cannot sell enough Twigs, you make no money and your business collapses. You need to know your customers, if Twig is the right product, and if you will have it in the right time, place, and quantities for your customers. However, Twigs come from trees, and the more you harvest the less you have to sell. Therefore, you need to establish a value for twigs that will drive replanting and support resource management. Since your customers need that product or service, how much they will pay for it and how we educate and show them its true value is the challenge we face as business leaders.

Chapter 4: Trends and Alternatives

Translating value into financial success today is more dependent on government and business collaboration than at any time in the past. This is because government, with the Great Recession, has taken on the role of lender of last resort. While successful businesses do not require government bailouts, they do need bureaucrats and politicians to understand how business really works in order to facilitate and support change. Business also requires communication from politicians to citizen stakeholder groups so consumers and workers can understand why changes are required. Without this collaboration, while businesses can strive to make greater profits, we will be sub-optimizing society. Today more than any time in the past since the Greek city-states, cities are the places were people work and spend their lives. From New York to Los Angles, Toronto, Beijing, Paris, London, Mexico City, Shanghai, Hong Kong, Berlin, and Sydney, the list goes on and on. These cities and their citizens are all dependent on the distribution of products. Every item a citizen buys, from food to clothes to toys, travels via a business or is formulated and packaged by a business. Since we cannot return to small, subsistence-level farms, government support for city infrastructure and business are critical if we want to change.

Recently I was at a meeting with metropolitan officials and industry leaders reviewing how the two sides could together address city and citizen concerns so industry could continue to grow. What stood out to me from the meetings was how little business and governments understood each other's capabilities and constraints. To me, a key question asked of the business panel was how a city planning department could create a worthwhile plan given business needs and the many changes that are taking place today. While not on the panel, my response to that question was to recommend Strategic Flexibility, which can aid cities, governments, and businesses in addressing the challenges we face. We need a strategic perspective in such forums and in planning departments. We need to review not just, existing programs but new concepts, which while requiring open dialogue and citizen involvement will result in more significant beneficial change.

Michael E. Raynor, who discusses the concept of Strategic Flexibility in his book, *The Strategy Paradox*, recommends that managers address multiple futures by formulating many choices. Using examples from Sony, Microsoft, Vivendi, and Johnson & Johnson, he shows how even with the best-laid plans, a change in the business environment can drive failure. Companies plan to do their best—no company plans to fail. We all aim for success, but the future has many challenges for which we are often not prepared. Raynor refers to a 1985 study that found, "the level of disagreement among top management team members about key environmental variables and strategic goals is positively related to firm performance."[48] This is in opposition to the need for consensus among the operational and functional management team where consensus is positively correlated with success. Raynor recommends that the corporate level not develop strategy but build "a set of investments that reflects disagreement about what the future holds."[49] The management team should then develop the strategy to address these alternatives. Steps in Strategic Flexibility include, anticipating the future and trying to account for all the relevant uncertainties. Formulating the best strategies and their core elements. Accumulating options and validating them and operating and managing your portfolio of options.[50]

Helping you to anticipate the future while formulating appropriate strategies is one of the objectives of this book. However, while none of us can predict with any degree of certainty what another person will do, we can statistically approximate how larger populations will react. Since we now interact in and live in a networked world, if we can affect enough of the networks, we can alter the present to achieve a better future, or we can let the future break us. In this book, I have identified seven broad future trends, summarizing one to five below and providing more comprehensive details in chapter 9.

Major Trends

Trend 1: Climate Change
Trend 2: The End of Environmentally Low-Impact Oil
Trend 3: Water Crisis
Trend 4: Population and Aging
Trend 5: Food Crisis
Trend 6: Flawed Economics, Accounting, Easy Profit vs. Value Profit
Trend 7: Civilization in Resource Conflict

Trend 1: Climate Change

Civilization and Climate[51] was a great title for E. Huntington's book on the impact of climate on weather. However, we could refer to the present situation as a clash of consuming civilizations as we have started to take our consumption patterns to an extreme. In 1979, the US National Academy of Scientists Climate Research Board convened an ad hoc study group on carbon dioxide and climate. The ad hoc group created the Charney Report on carbon impact on climate. They assessed a doubling of carbon as having a 3-degree impact plus or minus 1.5 degrees Celsius. Today, one of the most publicized and documented sources on climate change, although one facing increasing debate between proponents of a climate change extreme case and those supporting a lesser climate change scenario, is the

United Nations Intergovernmental Panel on Climate Change (IPCC). To understand the IPCC reporting, you need to understand that climate change and its challenges are based on climate change theories and modeling. While no one can say whether an individual weather event is caused by climate change, the fourth IPCC report did make it clear where the report writers stood on the subject of global warnings. They stated,

"Warming of the climate system is unequivocal, as is now evident from observations of increases in global average air and ocean temperatures, widespread melting of snow and ice and rising global average sea level."[52] The question is what this then means for your business. Do you:

> Do nothing, continuing our present ways of operating and hope the global outcome is favorable?
>
> Try to stabilize our growth at present levels and hope the outcome is favorable?
>
> Try to stabilize or control the climate or other factors so we can control the impact as we grow?
>
> Work to set the climate and environment back to a level which is more conducive for people?

Kyoto and Copenhagen tried to address climate change, but nothing really changed as the message and the objective was confusing. There is controversy about global warming causes, facilitated by Climate-gate, where people discuss the warming or non-warming of the world. For example, my wife and I had dinner on New Year's Day as we always do, with two conservative friends—a medical doctor and a chemical engineer, two of the smartest people I know. We agreed on many issues such as the population, food, and oil. However, when climate change and Climate-gate was brought up, there was a fierce debate. The reality is Climate-gate is about whether carbon is affecting the atmosphere, not about the fact that weather patterns are changing. The UN World Meteorological Organization publishes a report every year, a summary of some of the comments from the 2008 report are below.

Drought *At the end of July, most parts of the south-east of North America were classified as having moderate to exceptional drought conditions, based on the United States Drought Monitor. The continuous dry conditions across northern and central California resulted in numerous large wildfires. In Canada, southern British Columbia experienced its fifth driest period in 61 years.*

Extreme storms and flooding *In January, 1.3 million square kilometres (km2) in 15 provinces in southern China were covered by snow. Persistent low temperature and icing affected the daily lives of millions of people who suffered not only from damage to agriculture, but also from disruptions in transport, energy supply and power transmission. 2008 was one of the top 10 years for tornado-related fatalities (123) since reliable records began in 1953. According to statistics, 2 192 tornadoes were recorded during the year, well above the 10-year average of 1 270. The most deadly tropical cyclone recorded in 2008 was Nargis, which developed in the North Indian Ocean and hit Myanmar in early May, killing more than 70 000 people and destroying thousands of homes.*

Six consecutive tropical cyclones (Dolly, Edouard, Fay, Gustav, Hanna and Ike) made landfall on the United States, and a record of three major hurricanes (Gustav, Ike and Paloma) hit Cuba. Hanna, Ike and Gustav were the deadliest hurricanes of the season, causing several hundred casualties in the Caribbean, including 500 deaths in Haiti.

Arctic sea-ice extent during the 2008 melt season dropped to its second-lowest level since satellite measurements began in 1979.

For the first time in recorded history, the navigable deep-water routes of the fabled Northwest Passage over the top of North America, and the Northeast Passage over the top of the Russian Federation, were simultaneously free of ice.

Regardless of the causes, we are facing climate, water, and food obstacles as we near the end of easy oil. Many scientists agree on these challenges, and even those who do not agree on the cause don't disagree that there is a potential issue. So, if we can agree on that point, we need to examine cooperative business and government solutions. However, increasingly the most strident voices promote large-scale government intervention. The US capitalist model based on demand and supply is increasingly taking a back seat. This is dangerous for business, as governments will respond with increased taxes to address the issue, like the BC carbon tax in Canada or with cap and trade. The democratic capitalist model, like the Soviet model, will fail unless we find creative answers to today's problems as business leaders. So let's examine our next challenge.

Trend 2: The End of Environmentally Low-Impact Oil

Climate change, as we reviewed before, is a key driver in the push to reduce the amount of energy consumed from carbon sources. However, climate change is not the only driver. The end of easily accessible oil is also a factor, as are the forecasts on what the price for oil will be in the coming years. My department's role in one of the world's largest companies included tracking the cost and price of diesel and oil, not because we bought oil to sell to consumers but because everything we moved, everything we touched and sold required an expense in oil and diesel. Every product you see in a store requires fuel to move it, whether by ship, rail, or road, and that consumption comes at a hefty price. Below is the energy use in the United States. As you can see, 28 percent of energy is used for transportation.

Table 5   **Share of Energy Used for Transportation, 2008**

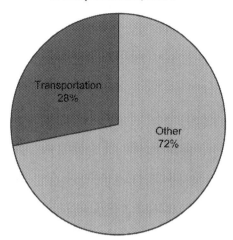

Source: Energy Information Administration
Annual Energy Review 2008.

Our Value Chain was built on being able to move raw materials and resources to fixed manufacturing locations and then distributing products from those locations to the cities, which have become our consumption nodes, and to rural areas. We have built a networked society where the population involved in farming has dropped as the cities have grown dramatically. "Between 1950 to 1980, in countries everywhere, more than a billion people migrated from rural areas to cities."[53] This model of consumption nodes, while supporting the increase in energy efficiency and reducing distribution costs, also means that we are increasing the amount of food moved from the country to the city. It means that as we have shifted jobs and production to China's manufacturing cities, our global economy has become heavily dependent on easily accessible, low environmental-impact energy, which we define as energy extracted from global oil resources where the environmental impact at extraction is minimal compared to other sources. This does not mean that I am a peak-oil theorist. However, the data peak-oil theorists provide and that of conventional sources such as the IEA appear to be starting to converge. To offset the decline in oil discovery and extraction, oil companies have now moved to water-intensive processes such as tar sand extraction and shale oil extraction, both requiring significant amounts of fresh water utilization.

Trend 3: Water Crisis

Fresh water is a subject that should be close to the stomach and heart of everyone, especially businesspeople. Take your average hamburger—it requires 2,400 liters, or 630 gallons, of water to produce.[54] As the water shortage accelerates, it will affect the amount of meat that we consume. According to the World Bank, more than 1.1 billion people do not have access to safe fresh water, and 2.6 billion do not have access to basic sanitation. There is a project called the Millennium Project to address water. However, many of the issues affecting water are not restricted to sub-Saharan Africa but affect countries from the United States to China. The driver behind the coming water crisis is our civilization's consumption requirement and the poor utilization we have made of land, which now requires intense water use, causing the decline in water levels. The world is mostly water. However, only 3 percent of the water on the earth is fresh, and 97 percent is salt water, which is undrinkable unless desalinated. The majority of the fresh water in the world resides in the United States and Canada. However, parts of the world are running out of water, including the Midwestern United States, China, Africa, the Middle East, and sections of South America. The crisis in water first came to my attention during my tenure at one of the world's largest farming co-ops. A core fact was that the massive drought that Australia has been experiencing for years reached the point that it had affected the global dairy farming industry and was driving a global price increase. From a short-term perspective, higher world milk prices were a positive, as it would result in higher prices. However, it was also a negative, as it drove farmers to sell their milk production at a higher cost. To consumers, the drought's result has been all negative, no upside. The prices of milk powder, milk, and cheese have increased, resulting in higher prices especially for the poor in developing countries who buy dried milk products. Less milk for poor children in their early growth means less effective workers and thinkers in a changed economy where a country's prosperity is linked no longer just to manual labor but to the innovative and creative nature of their population.

Water pollution is also a factor. In the US, as a *New York Times* investigation of water pollution records,[55] "showed the Clean Water Act were violated more than 506,000 times since 2004, by more than 23,000 companies and other facilities, according to reports submitted by polluters themselves." Violations ranged from failing to report emissions to dumping toxins at levels that might contribute to illnesses. The vast majority of those polluters escaped punishment (visit www.nytimes.com/toxicwaters). In addition, the *Times* interviewed more than 250 state and federal regulators, water-system managers, environmental advocates, and scientists. That research showed an estimated one in ten Americans was exposed to drinking water failing to meet federal requirements. The pollution of water and access to fresh water is a problem. In addition, we face a problem with ocean water, as dead zones have been created, affecting marine life.

Trend 4: Population Growth and Aging

Fourth, the world's population is forecasted to be 9.3 billion by 2050, after adjusting for the decline in birthrates at the first half of the twenty-first century. While birthrates have declined in western countries, they have also slowed globally. This will not, however, prevent the world's population from increasing to 9.3 billion. Unfortunately, given our present consumption patterns, the planet cannot sustain population levels much above present without significant changes in the way we do business. Population predictions do have errors based on migration, fertility, life span, disease vectors,[56] and changes in culture. However, the fact remains that the world's population is set to change significantly. In sixteen years, the world's population will be 8 billion people, a 1.3 billion increase. This growth will tax world resources. At the same time, Western countries will need to increase immigration to compensate for the decline in the birthrate of the European-descended population. Our world will be transformed to a mosaic of color over the next thirty years as European family birthrates continue at low levels and migrants' relatively higher birthrates take hold. This diversification in population will come at the same time as family sizes decrease and populations age, which will present unique challenges in North America and Europe.

Population growth and aging is a great opportunity for companies to drive profitability if they move away from disposable products, instead innovating and building products that last while meeting consumer needs. If we build value-added, long-lasting products, recycling and reuse will mean something. If, however, we continue to use the present capitalist model of credit and cheap products, we will not be able to feed and clothe the population at anywhere close to the level of the marketing plans our companies are utilizing. We must stop promoting a cheap, unsustainable lifestyle, and this is most true in the area of food.

Trend 5: Food Crisis

Given a rising population, we will require the equivalent of another 2.1 billion acres of arable land, an area the size of Brazil, to feed the population.[57] If you review the numbers, by 2026 we will be at 8 billion people. All of these people will need to eat. This means we need to review where we can produce food, the types of food we produce, and the value we place on different types of food. The food industry itself will have to change. The impact of large-scale production will need to be reviewed, as so much of our food is produced on large-scale farms requiring massive amounts of pesticide and fertilizer. These large quantities of pesticide and fertilizer pollute water resources and contribute to unsafe water conditions. So, we need to find a balance between increased food output and pesticide and fertilizer needs. We also will need to adjust the level of protein consumption that takes place. To understand the impact food will have, an excellent and fascinating read is *The End of Food* by Paul Roberts.

The history of food is important, as we can see historically what will happen as populations increase while land areas decrease. Thomas Malthus first proposed in his 1798 "Principle of Population" that food production could only increase arithmetically, while population would increase geometrically. Paul Ehrlich, in his book, *The Population Bomb*, revisited Malthus' ideas that population would exceed food production at some point and global starvation would occur. Population growth has taken place, though the impact has been overcome by changes in food and technology. The challenge now is that we have reached a level where we are seeing diminishing returns with our present application of technology.

Alternatives

In chapters 5 and 6, I will cover trends 6 and 7 and provide strategies to address the issues we face. Since we started by discussing Strategic Flexibility, let's review some tactical and strategic options. Important to note is that business and government Value Chain and supply chain offerings are customer and citizen dependent, driven by what business and government believe people want. While some of the following ideas will seem like high-tech ideas to government officials, all of the technology to achieve the ideas below are presently available, we only need the well to implement them.

Business and Government Tactics

Below are some processes that can reduce your footprint and save dollars at the same time. The words in parentheses are there to help you know if it is relevant for business or government.

Alternative Work Arrangement (Business and Government)

Given computer and telecommunications today, we have the ability with video phones and high-speed access to reduce required office space by telecommuting or outsourcing the work. This also allows access to a greater talent pool as well as addressing the impact of transportation as people are encouraged to work from home.

An alternative is in local areas, we can look at building utilization models using office pooling. Government and businesses with available space in this model would identify areas in buildings that they can sublet on a daily basis so that people living in one side of the city can utilize semi-public cubicle space closer to home rather than traveling twenty to thirty miles to the office. When proximity allows for teams of five to ten to get together, a configured office environment could be created amid a larger common workspace. This would allow for people from the same company to develop relationships within a team culture while still reducing space use. This type of coordination would require business support, but it addresses some concerns with working offsite.

Packaging Redesign (Business and Government)

Packaging redesign eliminates and reduces packaging and decreases space utilization and resource consumption. This results in a smaller warehouses footprint and lower transportation costs. An example is powdered detergent packaging reduction. Unilever challenged the category by compressing the air from the product so consumers could get the same number of washes from a smaller box of detergent. Less corrugate was required, and a lot more boxes were moved for fewer dollars. Next, liquid-concentrated products reduced the content so that the retail pack could be smaller, requiring less plastic. Packaging reductions for thousands of products, from shaving cream cans to cereal boxes, soup bars and other items, will save companies billions and reduce environmental impact.

Product Redesign (Government and Business)

Product redesign can eliminate billions in costs and resource use for even standard products. To accomplish this, however, we need the will. Take pop cans and bottles. You can buy pop in cans that are refrigerated at the counters at grocery stores or gas stations, which are where companies make the most money, or buy it in cans at grocery stores. Products purchased in aluminum cans and plastics bottles utilize resources in space, can and bottle manufacturing, electricity, and distribution. Alternatively, pop companies can redesign the product, offering to create franchises to sell mix machines to consumers like the mini-coffee machines Nestle has created in Europe for coffee. Small paper or plastic envelopes or containers could replace aluminum and steel cans, allowing for easier distribution and the removal of entire fleets of trucks from the road. The machines would be licensed and sold like photocopiers as product revenues increased due to a lower cost structure. The technology for the mix already exists, as do the machines, as restaurants use versions of this technology. The major impact, however, would be on labor, as this would involve a major transition in staff. However, this staff could be utilized in boutique franchises embedded in department stores to sell these products and other drink solutions pop companies can create and market at the higher end to compete with wine and beer sales. Staff could also be utilized in making the machines and maintaining them. A disruptive market change like this would drive other changes in resource reduction. See Curitiba's example for what can be accomplished when people decide to act.

Product Proliferation, Discontinuation, and More Efficient Business Models (Business and Government)

Companies introduce thousands of new products annually as they target more defined markets, offering diverse choices via small changes in product design. This item proliferation, when due to a small change, increases product costs across entire global supply chains. In one company, we reduced items by six hundred in a year and a half and still had more to go. The reduction reduced costs and improved performance. However, this needs to be done in line with profit plans, as companies then have to accept the product write down and disposal costs. To make this a truly beneficial act and increase the speed of change, governments need to adjust the anti-competition acts and create business exchanges so businesses can share their plans on an exchange and sell off the customer demand they do not want. In this way, all companies benefit as very small demand is moved to other businesses to take care of on larger production lines. The company discontinuing the items would get a benefit for providing advance notification of the business change.

Retail Sales Models and Product Demand (Business and Government)

We need to move to the next step in Collaborative Planning and Forecasting and take forecasting to a customer level. There are chains where you can order, pay for, and then pick up items in the store or get home delivery. Ecom businesses allow you to do this online. We can take this consumer purchasing process to the next level. Allowing customers to order the items online, pay, and designate the store for pickup while still allowing flexibility in the shop for specific items to be tested. In this way, product demand is directly linked to a customer and a store. This gives the customer freedom to shop as they would like but gives the retailer direction on what to stock where and when. Lead-time would be the key ingredient to making the process a success. A standardized retail process requiring customers to order twenty-four to forty-eight hours ahead of time, with longer lead times for higher-priced items, would reduce costs. Out-of-stock products and throws (items dumped in the garbage or marked down) would be reduced while allowing stores to level out buying decisions using price discounts, effectively reducing the actual cost benefit of supply chain predictability at the store level. This would also reduce store sizes, transportation costs, and the amount of concrete used to build. What is stopping us is, instead of retailers competing on the factors that matter, such as product quality, place, and price, Ecom and even bricks-and-mortar stores use shipping lead-time as a competitive advantage. The reality is consolidating millions of products over a two to three-day ship window will reduce the cube utilization of the trucks and decrease fuel costs and business costs while providing a benefit for the customer, who may not be even home for the delivery or who may delay the store visit for one to two days. This is where any of the three levels of government working with corporate alliances or on their own could standardize generic industry offerings in an area. This would provide consumers and businesses with set choices that would reduce the costs of business and pollution and waste while benefiting consumers. Really, is getting a book one day earlier freedom, or is it just liberal capitalism that will only drive your prices up?

Changes such as those proposed above would also create a much better loyalty program. Customers picking up an order in your store are much more likely to buy other items. We have the technology to make this an intelligent network, providing information to vendors in direct feeds. The key to making this work is not the technology, which we have today, but the marketing communication of the benefits to customers and governments and the will to implement. Cities implementing steps like this would not need massive projects to affect change but rather meetings between companies and agreement on consolidation days for customer orders. Changes like this in conjunction with the other tactics could reduce the number of trucks on the road by 15 percent to 20 percent, as most trucks now are not fully utilized given the diversity of order days of companies and customers.

National or Alliance-Driven Backhaul Markets (Business and Government)

A national network selling backhaul services would also facilitate reducing the miles trucks traveling empty. This program could be government supported or, even better, linked in with the mail service to start developing alternative business models for Postal Services. An example of this is GS1 and VICS, which introduced VICS Empty Miles in the United States and Canada. It is a web-based, shared-software service that allows shippers with loads to find carriers with excess backhaul or front haul capacity. It has the potential to be both an economic and environmental win. US retailer Macy's and carrier Schneider National have been using Empty Miles in partnership. Since GS1's debut, Macy's has added thirty backhaul truckloads per week, and while opening new lanes, saved the company approximately US$25,000 in transportation. The partnership has reduced emissions by more than two hundred tons and increased Schneider's backhaul revenue by 25 percent on some accounts. After the launch of Empty Miles in the United States, several Canadian companies including Rona, XTL Logistics, Fortigo Freight Services, and Hudson's Bay Company (HBC) participated in a proof-of-concept pilot. The Empty Miles service is delivered through a members-only web portal. Shippers have the option of using a special calculator to help define the potential ROI benefit from participating and reductions in carbon emissions.[58]

Driver Training Programs or automated driver controls (Business and Government)

A badly trained driver can impact fuel use by up to 30 percent, so better training for drivers, along with software to control the speed and braking of a vehicle, can have a significant benefit.

Idling Programs (Business and Government)

Implement a truck and car idling program in your distribution center, plant, or office parking lot.

Vehicle Fuel Tracking (Business and Government)

Automotive and Truck manufactures have the ability to track the fuel use and efficiency of each vehicle. This information can then be downloaded for asset management these uses of computerization can aide business in identifying and reducing the costs of truck and automotive movements. It can also aide governments to apply taxes and identify what types of fuel are actually being used. A key challenge in the area however is that each OEM has their own process for calculating field efficiency. Instead, all companies should use one calculation so comparisons on efficiency can be made. This change will help with engine development as companies can then see the impact of innovation in real world situations.

Leadership in Energy and Environmental Design (LEED)

The design of new buildings will have a dramatic impact, as between 2000 and 2030 over one hundred billion square feet of residential and office space will be built in the US.[59]. Indoor air quality standards will affect the products put into these new buildings.

Computer Recycling Programs (Business and Government)

Some companies such as Apple have redesigned their computers to reduce waste and have specific recycling programs for computers. Apple for example has instituted recycling programs in 95 percent of the countries where their products are sold, diverting more than eighty-three million pounds of equipment from landfills since 1994. In

2008, Apple recycled thirty-three million pounds of electronic waste, achieving a worldwide recycling rate of 41.9 percent. To calculate this rate, Apple used a measurement that assumes a seven-year product lifetime. Apple is committed to achieving an industry-leading recycling rate of 50 percent by 2010.[60]

We need programs such as this across electronic and other business to ensure continual benefits from reusing resources.

Designated Truck Lanes in Cities (Government)

Some cities have designated bike lanes and automotive lanes for cars with two or more people. These lanes are used mainly in morning and evening rush hours. A much better use would be to have specific lanes designated as truck lanes for specific times to allow traffic to move faster so we do not have large vehicles stuck in traffic. This would also make the roads safer for all traffic, not just the few. Biking is also very important, and since so few people actually walk, we might be better to split the sidewalk and designate a portion for bikes, allowing them to come completely off roads, making the roads and sidewalks safer for everyone.

The city of Curitiba is the best example of a city where bus traffic has been transformed. "The bus system of Curitiba, Brazil, exemplifies a model Bus Rapid Transit (BRT) system, and plays a large part in making this a livable city. The buses run frequently—some as often as every ninety seconds—and reliably, and the stations are convenient, well designed, comfortable, and attractive. Consequently, Curitiba has one of the most heavily used, yet low-cost, transit systems in the world. It offers many of the features of a subway system—vehicle movements unimpeded by traffic signals and congestion, fare collection prior to boarding, quick passenger loading and unloading—but it is above ground and visible. Around 70 percent of Curitiba's commuters use the BRT to travel to work, resulting in congestion-free streets and pollution-free air for the 2.2 million inhabitants of greater Curitiba. The popularity of Curitiba's BRT has effected a modal shift from automobile travel to bus travel. Based on 1991 traveler survey results, it was estimated that the introduction of the BRT had caused a reduction of about 27 million auto trips per year, saving about 27 million liters of fuel annually. In particular, 28 percent of BRT riders previously traveled by car. Compared to eight other Brazilian cities of its size, Curitiba uses about 30 percent less fuel per capita, resulting in one of the lowest rates of ambient air pollution in the country. Today about 1,100 buses make 12,500 trips every day, serving more than 1.3 million passengers—50 times the number from 20 years ago. Eighty percent of travelers use the express or direct bus services. Best of all, Curitibanos spend only about 10 percent of their income on travel—much below the national average."[61]

Long Combination Vehicles (Business & Government)

Long combination vehicles can significantly address carbon footprint, fuel use, and costs. However, given the limitation of some roads and corners, we should also look at longer articulated trailers that would be bigger than fifty-three feet but not as large as a LCV. The issue here is that politicians are concerned with consumer and citizen reaction, although data has shown that when operated properly, LCVs are safer.

Warehouse and Plants Floor Loading Trailers (Business)

Floor loading trailers outbound to stores can have as significant financial benefit for retailers but also for manufacturers. However, in some cases, the companies are unionized and the costs may outweigh the benefits. This is where private business can establish reload centers in cities for floor loading freight to warehouses. Another option is if the unload is at a DC and the floor load is on slip-sheets, grippers can be used to aid in unloading.

Slow-Steaming Ocean Ships (Business and Government)

Reduce the speed of shipping to drop costs, damage to ocean systems, and fuel use.

Containers as Bulk Shipping Units (Government and Business)

Today, grain is shipped in bulk container ships. However, many containers go back empty to Asia. We should be able to utilize the containers so we can load and unload grain in the same containers, using a new loading and unloading system. This would eliminate bulk grain ships. Presently, twenty-foot containers are shipped to Japan with specialty grains, but this could be significantly expanded.

Foldable Ocean Containers (Business and Government)

Containers today have to be moved on the rail and pulled by trucks to their destinations, and many return empty to their point of origin. Minimizing the space such containers occupy on trains and ships would be beneficial. There have been a number of collapsible containers designed, and finalizing a specific design to a global standard would reduce the impact on costs and the environment.

Buyer Training Programs in Buying Environmental Products (Business and Government)

An example is Office Depot, which trained buyers in buying more sustainable products.[62] Buying environmentally friendly products and training buyers in the programs available, such as Energy Star, Green Steal, Organic, and LEED, are important steps to take. Walmart is also motivating its vendors to be greener with its Sustainability 360 program. "Wal-Mart's initiative to work with suppliers to reduce packaging by five percent by 2013—an effort that will be equal to removing 213,000 trucks from the road, and saving approximately 324,000 tons of coal and 67 million gallons of diesel fuel per year. The company's goal is to develop partnerships that help suppliers run more sustainable businesses and factories."[63]

Cold Water Air Conditioning

Air conditioning is desired in hot climates and requires electricity to run. Yet, the one of the oldest air conditioning systems in the world, believe it or not, was built by King Herod,* the same King Herod you can read about in Bible stories. In King Herod's case, he used cold air from the desert floor to cool his palace. Enwave of Toronto has utilized the same heat exchange theory and by using cold lake water is reducing the electricity needed to cool buildings in Toronto through heat exchange principles. Enwave's Deep Lake Water Cooling (DLWC) is the world's largest lake-source cooling system, it reduces electricity use "eliminates 79,000 tonnes of carbon dioxide annually—the equivalent of 15,800 fewer cars on the streets of Toronto. Cuts 45,000 kg of polluting CFC refrigerants. Saves more than 61 MW of electricity annually—the equivalent power demand of 6,800 homes. Eliminates the need to install cumbersome, expensive equipment and to dispose of it at the end of its useful life."[64]

Roof Color Moving to White Roof Technology
(Business and Government)

White roofs are a building design criteria allowing for better Heating and Air Conditioning control which we need for increased energy management.

Hydrogen Cell Use for Buildings (Business)

Hydrogen cell use for buildings and for material-handling equipment such as the GenDRive for tow motors.[65]

Utilizing Roofs for Solar Power Generation
(Government and Business)

California and Ontario are two areas in North American where government is supporting solar energy panel installation on building which will attach and provide power to the electrical grid. This solar option is worth reviewing and needs to be designed into city and energy plans, as building use needs to be confirmed for a specific number of years to yields any payback.

Green Philosophy and Design

Rather than detail the changes and the possibilities here, my recommendation is to read *The Green Workplace*[66] by Leigh Stringer, which is a great book on greening your workplace.

Supplier and Vendor Programs (Business and Government)

Strategic Sourcing can be a critical driver of Continual Sustained Growth when utilized in business and in and across business alliances. Strategic Sourcing can deliver not only cost reductions but process improvements in industry when utilized to transition to shared facilities, trucks and manufacturing organizations leveraging volume for greater capacity utilization so resource needs are lowered. Take the automotive parts industry many companies need to buy steel and yet often they do so as individual companies, instead of as alliances. Alliances could improve the operational efficiencies of steel and plastic manufactures if production schedules and requirements are optimized.

Company Environmental Audit

Companies have started to identify processes to measure their carbon and environmental footprint categories. For example, Nike has had a carbon footprint done on parts of their business. Others measure water use, indoor pollutions, and energy use. These environmental audits, when incorporated into your company's policies, can allow for a developed strategy with measurements and actual percentages for improvement over time. Without measurements, we cannot tell if we are getting better or not, so having a valid audit done is a critical step.

Apple is a great example of an environmental assessment. They did an assessment using a comprehensive life-cycle analysis to determine exactly where their "greenhouse gas emissions—all 10.2 million metric tons of them1—come from.[67]

Simpler Ideas

Eliminate foam cups.

Reduce the height of coffee cup lids so less plastic is used.

Use low water use toilets and faucets.

Reduce travel (air and road).

Discontinue bottled water in the workplace and replace it with plastic reusable bottles.

Use double-sided printing.

Recycle company waste.

Adjust the temperature in your office, DC, and manufacturing plant down.

Buy offsets.

Buy electricity from alternative energy sources.

Use automatic light shut-offs.

Teleconference instead of traveling to a location.

Use electronic projectors in meetings to reduce printing.

Use a carpool program.

Move away from disposable cutlery in lunchrooms toward stainless steel or bamboo substitutes.

Buy Energy Star appliances.

Strategies

Standardized Packaging

One tactic we mentioned earlier was addressing your packaging on an individual-company basis. However, what is required is standardizing packaging and sizing across commodities and consumer-packaged goods. If we do not standardize, we are altering the competitive positions of companies that compete on product value versus product packaging. Instead of having, companies compete related to packaging, we need to standardize pack sizes and encourage competition on product benefits and service. We could still allow different colors and graphics while using a standard exterior. An example is shaving cream. We buy shaving cream in cans and then destroy them as most end in landfills. Companies could pack shaving soaps in very small, corrugate boxes instead. If we standardized the pack size, companies would be forced to compete on product value instead of incremental can sizes and the difference in nozzles. This change could be accomplished by business and government working together to set-up optimized standards using packaging alliances. Wal-Mart, is an example of a company who has taken this approach working with ECRM and Thumbprint Ltd., to create the Wal-Mart Stores Inc. Package Modeling software. This packaging software facilitates modeling materials and processes to improve the environmental impact of packaging. It utilizes a Consumer Meaningful Unit of Measure (CMUM) which is one serving, portion or use of a product.

We need to encourage competition based on a product's complete benefits and service to customers and the environment with sustainable packaging as one of the measures of success.

Cap and Trade

An example of a process that tries to both penalize and reward business to support business changes is the Cap and Trade Carbon system. This system, starting in 2005 at Kyoto, has grown from nothing to a three-hundred-billion dollar, soon to be multi-trillion–dollar, commodities market. Cap-and- Trade industries such as power generation, steel, and cement have limits placed on their emissions; and companies that go over their emissions can purchase emission reductions from those who are under their limit. Already-in-effect reductions for established industries and increases can be measured. However, the issue is offsets that can be bought from emissions reduction projects in developing countries. Tracking if the offsets are real is very, very difficult, as you are measuring something new, which never will happen, as the very function of the activity you are measuring is to provent an issue. Like the story of the emperor's new clothes. The emperor likes to buy clothes, and then a brilliant but unethical merchant comes along and convinces the emperor to buy clothes no one can see while he makes loads of money for selling nothing. The emperor is made to look like a fool while the people laugh and yet know that their taxes are paying for nothing but air. In the case of Cap and Trade, we will be paying for supporting a system that is almost impossible to monitor and which has already garnered billions for selling nothing. Presided over by the United Nations, who issues the credits, cap and trade requires a new profession of emissions assessors who work for a few large companies who have moved into the assessor businesses, such SGS and DNV.

This is an area fraught with issues. The issues with the process as identified by some, including Mark Shapiro in a *Harper's* article,[68] is that

> Just 60 percent of projects actually provided evidence that the CDM funding made a difference, and that 40 percent of companies would likely have reduced emission anyway … It turns out that overestimating reductions is the trapdoor in the offset system. Study after study has demonstrated that CDM's have not delivered the promised amount of emission reductions. According to a report by the U.N.'s Intergovernmental Panel on

Climate Change, the margin of error in measuring emissions from cement and fertilizer industries can be as high as 10 percent. For the oil, gas, and coal industries the margin of error is 60 percent; and for some agricultural processes, the margin of error can actually be 100 percent.

Instead of buying the emperor's new clothes of cap and trade, we need to look at alternatives, such as Usage Tax Reduction. If consumerism is driving increases in carbon, water shortages, etc., why not go to the source—the people? People buy and consume based on quality and price, so value products appropriately and provide tax reductions for products that meet a standard of need and resource utilization. If we do not work with the consumers, nothing will change. A system based on rewarding good behavior at the consumer level via building products with the right value and lower taxes can result in changes in consumer behavior.

Differentiated Marketing Strategies and Customer Service (Business & Governments)

Having implemented Differential Marketing Strategies[69] in the past, I know there are many opportunities with this process for defining the costumer we want to service and providing, making, and stocking what they want to buy. The key idea here is that marketing strategy is driven by the individual consumer potential profitability.

"Over a wide variety of packaged goods and soft goods categories 33 percent of category buying households account for at least 67 percent of category volume. This means that the top third of category buyers purchase at least three times as many boxes of cereal or pairs of blue jeans as the middle third and six times as much as the bottom third."

The majority of companies want to deal with the top third, as it is the most profitable. However, they also have to address the other segments, where Differential Marketing aids companies to focus their resources on satisfying their top segments. While simple, if the government would allow companies to sell to each other on an amortized basis customer demand for products they do not want to carry, companies could trade customers, allowing them to focus their strengths and allowing customers to know where to shop to get what they want. The customers, the companies, and the environment would benefit.

Transportation Companies (Business & Government)

Increased fuel costs have a dramatic impact on ocean rates. This has been leveraged by the Ocean Alliances that are facilitating cost increases in the hundreds of dollars, if not over a thousand, in ocean container rates. In the same way, road carriers, who have had their costs driven down and who have a fractured completive segment with low costs of entry, need to realize that a higher level of industry consolidation is required. Many carriers cannot afford the rates they are making, but all are awaiting the market's rebound—a rebound that when it comes will be limited in length. Road carriers need to get together, consolidate, and start to create not just regional carriers and national carriers but alliances as we have in the airline and ocean shipping industries. Given the investment in infrastructure required by LTL carriers, this process will aid them in the years ahead as fuel prices increase.

Government could also aid in this by restricting entry to trucking companies that have one hundred to two hundred standard trucks. This would drive consolidation of smaller shippers and increase efficiency while providing more flexibility and competition at the high end, as many large companies will not use carriers with only twenty to forty vehicles unless they provide highly specialized services. In addition, this would allow for greater freight consolidation, reducing pollution and shipping costs. While no one wants regulation back, we need a degree of control via licensing that presently does not exist.

Information Exchange (Business & Government)

There are terabytes of information on customers and vendors available, but privacy laws restrict access to this information. However, it is exactly this information, if parsed in the correct way, which would allow for significant changes in the way we interact with the environment. Trading of such information via the creation of confidential information business intelligence trading centers would allow for significant changes in the way we affect the environment. Since there is a valid concern on how data is used, governments should review creating a department like that of Statistics Canada, which is a government department in Canada that has statistical information access and control. Such a department could parse the information before licensing it to companies that would then be able to sell the data. The information would have all personnel content such as name, date of birth, and address removed and would be used to better design solutions. Consumers could also be allowed to sign on and sell access to their information to companies if they so desired.

Sustainable Cities (Government and Business)

A concept that is coming of age is the Sustainable city. On March 9th, 2009, Cisco signed a Memorandum of Understanding with Metropolis, an association of 106 of the world's cities, to develop its "Vision 2030" for sustainable cities. It is already building a fully wired city in New Songdo in Korea in conjunction with other companies. Based on the increase in population we will need hundreds of new cities. Cisco and other companies will be leading this build. Conceptually wired cities and the staff managing them can make intelligent decisions that will reduce our carbon emissions. Saudi Arabia has ordered four such new cities and China also has plans. IBM is also in this wired city sphere, but so far IBM's focus is on retrofitting existing sites. The key to success in my opinion is consumerism. We can have all the technology but we need to change the way consumers and workers who are all citizens interact with the environment.

Education (Government and Business)

All of the above ideas can work and will reduce our environmental footprint if we address the foundational area, education. The majority of people do not like change and react to challenges based on what we have in short term memory and the patterns of behavior and problem solving that worked in the past. Few of us are change agents who can visualize the need for change. Even fewer people can create a successful transformation plan. Education of the population is critical to an organizational and environmental change process, as you need to educate and train people in why a change is required and sell them on how it benefits them. Consumerism depends on convenience so we need to train ourselves and our children in the damage convenience can cause to the environment while identifying for business the profits that can result from changing this mindset.

The above ideas are only a few of many that can be implemented as we apply innovation to global challenges.

Chapter 5: Acknowledging the Challenges

Trend 6: Flawed Economics, Accounting, Easy Profit vs. Value Profit

In writing a book, you can make friends into enemies, enemies into friends, and create hatreds to last a lifetime, especially when discussing the economic impact of business on people. As a business leader, you face choices every day—choices on how your company treats others and what polices your company will follow. Unfortunately, too few business leaders give thought to the history of capitalism, Marxism, and the dialectic between the two that created consumerism. Adam Smith's ideas of capitalism and the invisible hand are as different from what we have today as is Communism in China from Engel's Communism. Instead, capitalism has morphed into consumerism, and the moral responsibility of government has been sacrificed on the altar of expediency. Conservatives are now those who require that government not legislate changes, and liberals today are those in favor of legislation. In reality, the US forces on both sides were responsible for the Great Recession, and cooperation between both sides will be required to solve the issues resulting from the recession and to support the health care system implemented by Obama's administration. This need for a new system is evidenced by Alan Greenspan's comments that the meltdown had revealed a flaw in a lifetime of economic thinking and left him in a "state of shocked disbelief."[70] Greenspan, eighty-two, acknowledged under questioning that he had made a "mistake" in believing that banks, operating in their own self-interest, would do what was necessary to protect their shareholders and institutions. Greenspan called that "a flaw in the model … that defines how the world works."[71] Coming from a past chairman of the Fed, this was a major concession and supports the view that present models are flawed.

Joseph E. Stiglitz, Noble Prize winner for *Freefall*,[72] makes clear why the present Walrasian economic models are not working and provides alternatives. He makes the point that two basic tenets of the Walrasian model are that behavior is based on self-interested preferences and complete and costless contracting.[73] Stiglitz's work with Bruce Greenwald answered questions on the results of the Walersian model and showed, "With perfect markets there was always full employment and with imperfect information there could be unemployment."[74] This is a key point, as it affects the conservative view that markets are efficient. If markets are, in fact, inefficient, problems would be ongoing, so governments should have a role in intervening in markets. This is a key point because the fight between liberals who promote green solutions and conservatives is often over the need for government intervention. As Stiglitz points out and as you can see in cases where governments have intervened, business actually became more efficient (Singapore and Korea are two examples). Many remain concerned in the United States, Canada, and Europe about the trillions in tax money poured in to stop the Great Recession. However, this move was the only way to stop a massive slide into a Great Depression. The key is balance between business dominance and government intervention. Since the Great Recession, governments have become the lender of last resort. We therefore need to open dialogue between business and government on the development of alternative economic models.

In America, Europe, and Canada, consumerism needs to be addressed, as in its present form it is driving long-term economic failure. Some economists would argue we need more consumption to get through the current economic recession. We do need consumption but a need-based consumer model rather than a want-based model. With the world population increasing to new levels, consumption will increase—it is the manner and degree of our consumption that is of concern. Want-based consumerism is a dynamic, symbiotic result of the desire consumers have for lower-cost products in the erroneous belief that it will benefit them while minimizing corporate shareholder profits. This consumer ethos has in fact led to few real benefits for consumers aside from cheap disposable products while narrowing corporate diversity, reducing employment, and increasing pressure on the poor.

This inequity is the driving force behind the creation of La Via Compesina, an international movement of peasants, small- and medium-sized producers, landless, rural women, indigenous people, rural youth, and agricultural workers.[75] Their objective is to defend the values and the basic interests of their members from sixty-nine countries from Asia, Africa, Europe, and the Americas. The reason this organization is important is that businesspeople usually neglect the history of capitalism, land ownership, corporate management, and our impact on people around the world. As corporate businesspeople, we think in terms of goals, objectives, profitability, and risk. La Via Compesina is the reaction of peasants in sixty-nine countries to the corporate actions taken to provide products to consumers and the resulting long-term degradation of the environment. Many business leaders have been trained to think in the short term, when today we need to think ten to fifteen years out as we face economic and environmental challenges.

In the next few pages, we reverse how we normally look at problems and approach them from an opposite perspective to see what we can learn using a reverse Strengths, Weaknesses, Opportunities, and Threats Analysis based on wanting, increased pollution, and poverty and what it means for the way business and government interact.

Reverse Disaster SWOT

Strengths of the existing mode for destroying the environment

Consumers do not want increased cost increases

Consumers do not want increased taxes

Consumers believe low-priced products are in fact cheap as the Natural Capital costs are not included

Consumers desire cheaper, less-expense products as they have lost wages and unemployment has increased

Business does not want increased taxes

Governments are not sure about the right approach

Climate change

The end of environmentally low-impact oil

Water shortages

Population and aging

Food crisis

Flawed economics

Third world countries require economic development, which is not presently sustainable if the West continues to consume at existing rates without innovating

What do we learn from this approach?

The majority of consumers do not understand what is happening and what it means for them.

Business wants increased profits or they lose shareholder value, and so do not want increased taxes.

Any business that changes before other businesses change is running a business risk.

Governments do not want to upset voters and businesses that support them, and so they want to minimize involvement.

Weaknesses

The problems are real, and sooner rather than later, consumers and businesses will be forced to act

When governments do act, they will be forced to increase taxes dramatically

Taxes on sales of goods

Taxes on wages

Taxes on business

Kyoto carbon trading has had a minor impact

Large corporations are using green washing as a marketing tool

Informed business leaders know there is a problem

Governments at all levels realize there is a problem but are unsure of how best to react given the numerous stakeholders

What do we learn from this approach?
Government needs to take a leadership position.
Business needs to act now to preempt government and legal ramifications once consumers and workers realize how serious the issues are.

Opportunities

Do not inform consumers about the complexity but keep the issues simple

Utilize consumer groups who know there a problem to suggest radical solution people will not like

Create a lack of leadership and country agreement

Increase economic problems as people cannot focus on the mid and long term when concerned about their jobs

What do we learn from this approach?
Consumers and citizens need to be educated on the issues
Consumers and workers need to be informed about the data on both sides, not based on political biases.
Leadership will be critical during the next ten to fifteen years.

Threats

Consumers learning more about how the economy and environment interact will affect government leadership and decisions
Decisions on the environment will affect business

What do we learn from this approach?
Governments need to support training for consumers so that they are part of the solution, not part of the problem.
Business needs to develop the tools to support informing consumers rather than having legislation pushed at them.

When you review the reverse SWOT above, you can see that we have somehow achieved almost all the items we need to exacerbate the problem, creating a drastic, unappealing, and economically catastrophic impact. We are like the *Titanic* streaming along with people playing music on the deck and looking at icebergs when we know there is a problem and that the majority of the problem is hidden but coming up fast. An example of a simple tool that for training consumers and citizens by the government is E2, a simple chart which shows that as economic resource utilization under present models increases, environmental sustainability decreases. The chart, shown in Table 6, is simple, as it depends on factors every consumer has seen around them as growth has expanded and land use has intensified.

Table 6

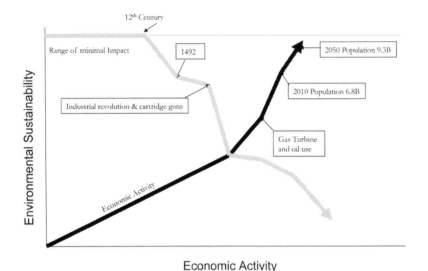

E2
Economic Activity + Environmental Sustainability

Companies focused on high resource utilization per item effectively increases environmental derogations. Let looks at some of the changes government will need to do if we do not implement an organized business and government-coordinated change process.

Unappealing Alternatives

Climate change

Cap and Trade
Common taxes on carbon emissions—"The way to do this is to have all countries of the world impose a common tax on carbon emissions (that is taking the externality of the emissions) or equivalent, a tax on oil, coal and gas at rates reflecting emissions they

generate when burned."[76] British Columbia has already implemented a carbon tax.

Trade sanctions raised against countries who pollute more than the rest of the world based on a standardized global emissions per person.

Water Shortage Changes

Management, coordination of a more efficient use of water
Offset and mitigate water demand
Include environmental costs in the rate structure to increase water costs[77]

Business penalties

Below are four examples of issues affecting business in the past. Contextualize these and think about what the government and the judicial system will do once problems escalate. Will government accept responsibility, or will you and your business be the target?

> British Petroleum—Gulf of Mexico oil spill resulting in still to be determined damage to US coastal areas. The company's image has been affected and so far they will be required to pay $20 Billion in damages to the people affected.
> Union Carbide and Bhopal—twenty thousand died, and some one hundred thousand were affected. The company's image was damaged, and the US government would not allow extradition of the CEO to India although a US$470 million payment was made.[78]
> WorldCom CEO Bernard Ebbers was sentenced to twenty-five years in prison for causing the largest bankruptcy in history up to that point.

Enron's former CEO, Jeffery K. Skilling, was sentenced to more than twenty-four years in prison. He was also forced to repay forty-five million dollars, which wiped out his fortune.

As the environment degrades, business costs and taxes will rise, and business leaders will be blamed if we do not accept business' social responsibility now. As corporate leaders, we must understand that the C-suite is responsible for what is manufactured, produced, and sold. Responsibility for disaster and for change resides with the leadership. Change can only happen if we accept responsibility and focus on:

- ✓ Environmental Proofing of our companies against environmental risk
- ✓ Changing marketing plans
- ✓ Innovating product design
- ✓ Business processes
- ✓ Government decisions

Challenges

Change can be driven by a variety of factors—internal and external—and the impact of the changes we make will be non-linear and complex. The majority of people working on sustainability have heard of James Lovelock, who advanced the Gaia Theory on the impact we are having on the globe. What many would not expect is a key point he raised in his latest book, *The Vanishing Face of Gaia: A Final Warning.*[79] I quote James Lovelock here, as in many ways the comments he makes are counterintuitive to the way we view the green movement.

I suspect that we worry less about global heating than about a global economic crash, and forget that we could make both events happen together if we implemented an immediate global 60 per cent reduction of emissions. This would cause a rapid fall in fossil fuel consumption and most of the participles that make the atmospheric aerosol would with weeks fall from the air. This would greatly simplify prediction and we could at last be sure that global temperature would rise; the removal of the pollution aerosol would leave the gaseous greenhouse unobstructed and free at last to devastate what was left of the comfortable interglacial earth. Yes if we implement in full the recommendations made at Bali within a year, far from stabilizing the climate it could grow hotter not cooler.

Lovelock is not advocating doing nothing. He is raising concern about the impact of many changes we have made to the earth. What we do know is that our time to address the changes is limited and any approach we take must balance the need for action with wisdom, as the earth is a functional, complex living system we know very little about. In addition, we must factor in a human perspective on urban air pollution, or PM particulate matter, which is the main driver. The World Bank provides estimates of annual average PM 10 concentrations in over 3,000 cities, and the WHO estimates 865,000 deaths in 2002 as a consequence of PM 10 in these cities (WHO 2007).[80]

Key to accomplishing change, as reviewed before, is the model proposed by Paul Hawken and the Lovins of the Rocky Mountain Institute and the inclusion of natural capital into the forms of capital we value. Again, the four forms of capital they identify are:[81]

Human Capital, in terms of labor intelligence, culture, and organization; financial capital—cash, investments, and monetary instruments; manufactured capital, including infrastructure, tools, and factories; and natural capital, made up of resources, living systems, and ecosystem services.

Incorporating natural capital into financial calculations will provide a more realistic pricing of the costs of our business production and growth. However, this still leaves the need for an accounting mechanism that will allow us to see profits in a new light. We propose that accounting standards start to factor into financial statements a different way of looking at profits. International financial reporting standards need to include a way to factor natural capital into profit calculations. With the utilization of IFRS standards by Canada in 2011, Mexico in 2012, and Japan in 2014, it is a key time to start reviewing a process and for companies to try out different options. While accountants debate such a change, our proposal is that companies start to include natural capital in their cost-benefit analysis, as it will increase their profitability now and encourage behavioral change. We define existing profit calculations that do not include natural capital as Easy Profits and calculations that include natural capital as Value Profits.

Easy Profit: defined as profit excluding natural capital costs versus

Value Profit: defined as profit after incorporating natural capital costs.

Easy Profits

Easy Profits destroy Natural Capital as companies' P&Ls do not include the impact on Natural Capital, so it leads to poor decision making. Most corporate managers focus on Easy Profits, which do not factor in the climate, water, energy, human costs consequences, and costs of the actions taken to achieve such profits. An example is companies that continue to market to consumers the idea that food and apparel costs can continue to decrease when such companies are not assessing the impact of their strategies on quality and health, competing only on price. An example of the impact of this approach can be seen in the way chickens have been bred. Paul Roberts, in *The End of Food*, reviews this: "Whereas a 1970's era broiler needed ten weeks to reach slaughter weight, today's model does it in forty days, which means an enterprising chicken farmer can raise two more crops each year and thus increase his annual output by 40 percent."[82]

The biggest problem Roberts identified when working with Dong Ahn, a researcher at Iowa State University, is chicken breeders have been so successful that "the rest of their anatomy can't keep up. Breast muscles grow so swiftly, that muscle cells don't fully form and cannot completely relax with the result that breast muscle often remains in a state of semi contraction which affects meat quality."

Low-price leadership is the place to be when you are large enough to drive competition down and mass production allows for healthy economics of scale. However, if your business is not machine-intensive but instead labor and animal-intensive, reducing costs does not give you the same cost reduction unless you reduce the value of the inputs. We know the present methodology to get continual price reductions are often at the detriment of the climate, water, energy, and human factors. So, we need to find a smarter way to make such decisions. Value Profitability is our recommendation for doing so.

Value Profitability

In our lives, only grand moments and terrible crimes tend to stand out, like streetlights in fog. Moments which enlighten or darken our lives, like clouds passing in front of the sun at sunset. The demolishing of the Berlin Wall, September 11, 2001, the Bali bombing, the invasion of Iraq, the killing of Uday and Qusay Hussein, the blackout across the Northeast and Hurricane Katrina are moments permitting one the opportunity to take off the blinders of daily life and expose oneself to the glaring light of harsh reality. The function of Value Profitability analysis is to focus a searchlight of information, like a stream of protons, on the contributing factors corporate officers and managers need to consider when making decisions. Value Profitability facilitates analyzing those decisions within a historical, social, environmental, and economic cost framework. This new cost framework will enhance accountability and make environmental choices relevant. Our challenge as people and leaders is to create a focus on Value Profitability, incorporating natural capital into our plans for our company and countries so we can address energy, water, and climate change issues, making them corporate brand concerns. On the Web, you can find carbon calculators, however, aside from government reports, it is difficult if not impossible to find a method and process for identifying the true value of a product and service versus its present price. However, having this information would facilitate you making better decisions. For example, some major companies track oil prices weekly and monthly and manage their supply chains by accessing and managing the impact of diesel prices on costs. This is a good investment and a strategic advantage, as managing fuel means you are managing costs and carbon. This allows you to increase profits and reinvestment in your business.

Take the blackout across the Northeast on August 14–16, 2006, as an example where the choice of not making ongoing value-added investments in an energy network, instead taking Easy Profits and treating energy as a commodity as opposed to a necessity, played havoc with power used by fifty million people. The consequences of choosing Easy Profits instead of Value Profits only came to be recognized in the middle of the two-day black out. This type of incident is a precursor to what the full consequences can be of our dependence on oil and resources which are non-renewable and which we are using up at an increasing rate.

Smartway, the US carrier process that rewards carriers that are more energy efficient, is one form of a program that is a start towards a Value Profitability process. Additional processes that would facilitate the government aiding business would be decisions on copyright and patent protection. The reality is companies only make sufficient profits for high-value items if they hold patents. Restricting patents on products that damage the environment is an economic and business method to facilitate appropriate resource decisions. The products that do not have patents may still be made, though manufacturers would receive less profit and therefore would have little incentive to continue to produce or invest.

Another process that would support value is the creation of innovation zones to access the benefits and value of up-and-coming disruptive technologies. Think about the technology war that occurred between Sony and Toshiba on HD-DVD. In that innovator war, as in the previous one between VHS and Beta, billions were spent on electronics that ended up in the garbage. Today, we have tools such as the Stage Gate Process that allow marketers to reduce the risk of poor products. However, there would be a significant benefit to developing innovator city competitions. Cities would be designated where the technology could be tried, and based on this a decision could be made as to what equipment was manufactured and where. Taking this approach would reduce investment in massive launches and dramatically reduce the waste in concurrent designs. It would also allow for a focused measurement of the environmental impact of technology before general release to the world.

Controlling innovation after general release is an onerous task. Managing innovation, on the other hand, would leave competing companies and the environment better off. This would require legislation and stronger patent laws, but it would benefit countries as key cities could be identified as test beds in major countries. An organization like the Olympic Committee could decide which countries get to test which inventions and set criteria for success.

Value Profitability supports the unique yet diverse concepts of capitalism, democracy, individual freedom, and pluralistic institutions. It combines those concepts with the need for a focus on family, stability, and environment. It can aid us in addressing the social and technical dislocation of workers before the aging population in the

West is required to face the increasing strength of developing countries with higher birthrates. In addition, resource development, supported by governments and businesses, is integral for the interaction and transaction of business in global society. Without resource security in water, food, and oil, countries will be forced to pull back from development and business competitiveness. If we win the martial battle in Afghanistan and Iraq and lose the battle in our homes for employment, freedom, and security, we will have been defeated. Since the "clash of civilizations" looks increasingly like it will be driven by environmental and resource conflict, applying Value Profitability will aid us in addressing these key issues.

Contributing Factors to Instability

September 11, 2001, Enron/WorldCom, the Internet business collapse, sub-prime mortgages, and the Great Recession are all results of immoral acts. These acts have very little in common on the surface, yet they have the same root cause—men and women who placed personal feelings, greed, and hate ahead of the pain they would cause others. Such persons do not consider the long-term consequences of their actions or, as in the case of Al Qaeda, consider dramatic consequences desirable. Consequences range from over 2600 people dying to hundreds of millions of people losing their investments, health, and having to spend years recovering from the personal loss to their families. Money that could have been invested to benefit the poor was wiped out along with millions of jobs.

Each of these acts was facilitated by the failures of government, corporate, financial, and democratic agencies to ensure the security of the individuals and companies that depend upon them. Christians say that the only security we have as individuals is in the cross of Christ, a security that is permanent and eternal. The security discussed here, on the other hand, is transitory, impermanent, and requires the constant vigilance of corporations and citizens. The threats to stability that we face today are different from threats faced during the Cold War, when the threat was Communism and nuclear war. During the Cold War, Mutually Assured Destruction (MAD) was adopted as a policy to combat the Communist threat. However, while the Capitalist and Communist systems never fought nuclear battles directly, they fought via non-nuclear proxy wars—small wars in which millions felt the consequences of battles between Eastern and Western blocs. Today, threats to peace remain as numerous as ever, though increasingly the largest threats come from leaders who place short-term company/personnel profitability ahead of long-term goals and consequences and governments, industries, and corporations pursuing short-term benefits and neglecting long-term negative consequences.

The general population now has little faith in business or political leadership. Part of the failure of corporate leadership is that CEOs spend a very short period at one company. Moving from one firm to another, CEOs develop little personnel loyalty to a firm, shareholders, or employees. Another contributor to leadership's shortsightedness is that many leaders are not well informed about the issues that are taking place today. This, along with a short tenure, gives CEOs minimal time to make changes while incorporating ethics and moral responsibility into their decision matrix. Instead, the focus is on Easy Profits, overlooking the long-term consequences on people and places. We need to change this and define capitalist leadership within the context of Value Profitability. Markets and production assets must be utilized so that we create customers and products good for the environment. For example, say I land on an island with ten thousand trees and I will be there for two years. An investment company offers me ten thousand dollars for every tree I sell them. I will clear all the trees for wood in the two years, and in the end, there will be no wood, no shade, and no food. If I am leaving the island in two years, this may not concern me. However, if, on the other hand, I know that I will be there five to twenty years, I will be more selective. Instead of clear-cutting, I will harvest trees while replanting others so I can start a tourism industry and harvest dead growth for export on a limited basis. If 50 percent of my bonus is short term and 50 percent of my bonus is based on long-term results, my decision process will be more focused on long-term development.

Utilizing Value Profits

Below is a chart showing present inputs into product pricing and suggested Value Profit elements.

Establishment of Value

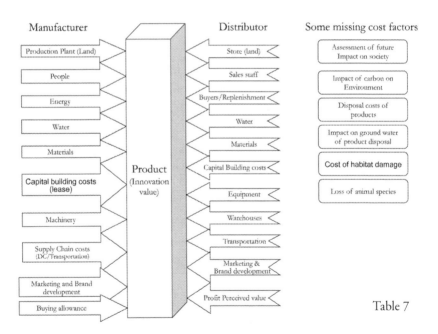

Table 7

To utilize Value Profits, two P&Ls will need to be created. One P&L will be the official one, while the second one, your Value Profit P&L, will incorporate a natural-capital cost element, allowing you to develop stretch goals as a business. While it is possible to actually do a net present-value estimate to identify what the Value Profit natural-capital input value would be (and we are attempting this valuation using World Bank, IMF, and other databases), for now we suggest you apply the percentages shown in Table 8 to the natural-capital inputs shown in Table 9.

Table 8

Year	Percentage
1	5%
2	10%
3	15%
4	20%
5	25%

Table 9

	Cost Elements
1	Water
2	Meat
3	Seafood
4	Cost of capital if land not developed for 100 years is used
5	Paper
6	Steel
7	Use of ingredients from animals identified as near extinct
8	Oil
9	Grain
10	Use of ingredients from plants identified as near extinct

You can have your accounting department create the Value Profit P&L and provide it to you along with your weekly numbers. Adding Value Profitability as an accounting mechanism allows us to focus our resources now, not only on reducing inputs that use Natural Capital, but also on implementing technology and options today that will address natural-capital costs. It will focus business departments such as marketing, design, manufacturing, supply chain, logistics, accounting, and finance on changing behaviors and adjusting the culture. It will also have an immediate impact on present profitability decisions. Take oil as an example. Based on adding an increase to the calculated price of oil and using the Value Profitability P&L to manage my operations, I will, in advance of the market in the area of transportation start to make decisions that will allow me to reduce oil costs now and increase present and even future profitability by:

- ✓ Implementing transportation technology for consolidating loads
- ✓ Floor loading
- ✓ Addressing packaging
- ✓ Increasing use of rail options
- ✓ Starting to work with rail companies to do rail delivery to stores where applicable
- ✓ Implementing many of the options listed in the earlier chapter

Incorporating Value Profitability will motivate you to make better decisions and facilitate your doing better long-term planning so that when fuel hits the higher price and water resources are less, you will be ready. The inclusion of natural capital into your P&L can start at 5 percent and move up from there. The amount you include will adjust the way you do business. The higher the percentage you use, the more incentive you will have to change and reduce your costs. In some cases, there may also be a capital investment required for example with packaging you may need new dies, with floor loading you may want to put in conveyors. These investments should go through a normal investment review, net present value and return analysis. When doing this you will need to show the impact without natural capital and with natural capital. In the end the savings you gain should make the decision clear even, without the natural capital impact.

While we are not suggesting adding the Value Profit number to your consumer pricing at present. However, you should start to consider a way to show this cost to customers. A suggested process is:

> Step 1: Show the environmental input. Timberland tries to do this by a sticker.
> Step 2: Show the Value Profit costs and real value number. Showing these costs to consumers will start to accustom them to the real costs of products before the actual price requires adjustment.

Reduced resource use and improved cost management will result from applying Value Profitability. However, we also need to look at other applications. Another application for Value Profitability is to increase employment in appropriate areas by utilizing the dollars saved throughout your value and supply chain to invest in innovation and business growth.

As we look ahead to the next few years from a business perspective, they will be tough. We are not yet out of the forest, and government debt repayment estimates range as high as $7 trillion for dollars that will need to be reimbursed due to the Great Recession.[83] While many think customers will be more conservative, we also live in an age that is technology driven. Rhodes and Stelter[84] and others view us as operating under Kondratiev waves—cycles in the world economy—dependent on cycles of innovation. These K-waves average fifty years in length, with cycles of alternating periods between high growth and periods of relatively slow growth. Today, we could be in the last phase of a wave. What we need now is innovation to move us out this wave. Nanotechnology, biotechnology, and energy technology are all options. Looking to the past at how companies addressed issues in other recessions may help focus on cost cutting, though we are in a new era, where cutting costs and selling more of the same resource-intensive use items will only accelerate environmental devastation.

While we must address costs, we need to do so in a different way by using Value Profitability and new strategies and tactics of integrating industrial data and standards and consolidating business units while utilizing funds for innovations in packaging, products, and processes around demand and supply. Utilizing existing technology in new ways can effect changes.

Incorporating Value Profitability allows us to establish a business stretch target for profitability improvements now. Larger companies think in five-year plans and delivering profitability consistently but the focus is often on this year and next. Very few leaders have on their agenda developing innovative solutions that will grow profits consistently over the long term. We are not trained to think in this way, which is why the attempts by companies to create sustainability reports is a challenge that usually gets put in the context of what a company can save or how it can increase profits by cost cutting using sustainability.

"Reporting on achievements in this area can enhance a company's public image but it also presents an opportunity for locating costly waste and inefficiency."[85]

Unless they work in private corporations, corporate officers are driven to make a greater profit in year or at the most over two years or they will lose their jobs. This creates, a drive to achieve higher Easy Profits fast, not a drive to sustainable Value Profits. However, as a business leader, you need to focus on how you can make Value Profits, not Easy Profits. The oil spill in the Gulf of Mexico by British Petroleum is an example of what happens when companies focus on Easy Profits. Often safety and quality are sacrificed at the altar of expediency.

Trend 7: Civilizations in Resource Conflict

We want to be safe, secure, have a house, and know our children can go to school and have a happy future. In other cultures, people want to know that their beliefs and views will be respected and not violated, that they can have food to eat and not starve, and that their children will not be excluded from the future. In America, the idea has held sway for many years that the best way to achieve this objective for the world is by exporting democracy and globalization. However, when Americans call for a world controlled by democracies, they mean, as pointed out by Amy Chu,[86] "Democracy for and within individual countries. That is we envision a world in which brutal and unjust dictatorships are replaced by freely and fairly elected leaders accountable to their citizens. We imagine ourselves, moreover, at the helm of such a world. As President Clinton predicted in his second inaugural address: 'The world's greatest democracy will lead a whole world of democracies.' By contrast, the last thing most Americans want is a true world democracy in which our economic and political fate is determined by a majority of the world's countries and citizens."[87]

The United States and the West has spent billions to promote democracy so that today 62 percent of all countries are democracies.[88] However, the most frequent result is a domination of majorities by despots who rise to power through the popular vote and then allow minorities to dominate local markets, which in turn yields terror and violence for those minorities. Elections in Iran have resulted in the election of racists, separatists, and, today, potential Islamic theocracies. Fareed Zakaria makes the case that while in the West liberal democracy go hand in hand, increasingly in the world, "democracy is flourishing; liberty is not,"[89] and he calls this phenomena "illiberal democracy."

This struggle for power was played out in the Americas with the establishment of the United States in the Revolutionary War against Britain, and the French revolutions were another aspect of this. Western civilization has had an extended period to understand and deal with the transfer of power from a few to the many. To define what is meant by democracy is important, however, as there is a tendency today to equate liberal capitalism (or market economic capitalist trading) with democracy (the rule of many).[90] This is very important because while democracy allows for liberal capitalism, liberal capitalism does not necessarily allow for democracy, as is the case in China. Even in the United States, arguments take place over whether capitalism and economies should be subservient to democracy, as opposed to democracy being subservient to capitalism. The debate of who should have control has taken place throughout the history of democracies. It becomes even more important today as power and wealth become increasingly concentrated in the hands of the elite in Europe and the United States that rarely interact with the majority. This is important because decisions will increasingly need to be made on how limited resources are allocated.

Today's political elite agendas increasingly conflict with the needs of democratic societies for security when the agendas impact foreign policy, an example of which is the oil industry's leadership, water, and food security. This is exacerbated as the power of the elites to affect policy determination has grown out of proportion to their population size.

Most managers or executives globally are not part of the elite, top 1 percent of the population, and they would not like to live in an environment where democracy does not exist. It is therefore contingent on corporate citizen managers to recognize that while short-term policies may create limited markets, the long-term goal should be to work with peoples and governments to create Value Profits that benefit three of the four pillars of present-day society—the people, the government, and corporations. We need to ensure that we promote policies for training workers and consumers in democracy, not just capitalism. This will increase stability while growing your market. If we don't take this approach, we will end up with a globalization where the vast majority of people fear and envy those who are financially and environmentally better off.

> In Southeast Asia's indigenous population majorities, global markets have produced multimillionaires, billionaires and multi-billionaires—but only among members of another ethnic group. As a result, despite marginal increases in their income, indigenous Southeast Asians often feel that free markets benefit only

"outsiders"—ethnic Chinese and foreign investors—
along with a handful of corrupt indigenous politicians
in their pockets.[91]

Issues such as in the above quote drive not only ethnic but also civilization
and culture violence and need to be planned for and addressed. It is
important that as we address the world's ability to support us that we
do not forget human threats. Governments and corporations need to
foster goodwill and promote security. We need a secure society that
also has freedom, for if we lose freedom we end up being the loser, not
only morally and socially but monetarily, as wealth gets concentrated
and the model on which we base profit generation is destroyed because
of a lack of balance. We need to ensure that the tools we use to address
environmental issues do not destroy what we seek to defend.

Applying theories globally of Western cultural superiority as we
draw nearer to 2030 will result in threats and violence from indigenous
counter-Western cultural movements as people get indigestion from the
failures of globalization. When disagreements come to the surface amid
Western economic oil requirements and special-interest groups seeking
their own interests and those of indigenous power elites and not the
greater interests of citizens and global trade, people may turn to war and
terrorism. From a business perspective, we need to position our business
so that we recognize and support countries' cultural independence and
respect their religions while not compromising or shortchanging our
own. While we may not agree with a culture's beliefs, as long those
beliefs do not result in violence to our peoples and societies, we should
seek understanding and tolerate them while as friends offering changes
that may be beneficial for their societies. In the context of our own
civilization, where pluralism is expected and allowed, their culture must
do the reverse, tolerating our pluralism as long as it is ethical and moral
and not attempt to demolish it.

Corporations need to promote and support ideas that move beyond
just selling products and start developing programs and products that

lessen and do not accentuate deeper cultural, economic, and religious issues while still focusing on sustainability. Corporations need to develop a holistic perspective and process that creates and promotes corporate interest groups that provide global concepts of cooperation that go beyond economic globalization. We need to recognize that there are many theories holding that globalization is a conspiracy of which multinationals, America, and Britain are a part. Such smoking-gun views are espoused by Michel Chossudovsky[92] and the Centre for Research on Globalization. While the United States was initially in Afghanistan to fight the Soviets and then Al Qaeda, it makes sense that there are also other reasons since "Afghanistan is essential for any country wanting to exercise its supremacy in Central Asia and has long been covered by Russia, the United Sates and above all by Saudi Arabia. In Washington it is considered the best transit zone for the extraction of Central Asia's petroleum and natural gas."[93] In my experience, most companies not connected to oils and minerals are dealing with the everyday reality that they need to stay in business and make a profit. Such a profit can only be made by creating global or regional brand strategies that take brands to the people that count—the customers of each country. For most of the world today, "there is no question that Nike, Gap, Reebok, Starbucks, Ben & Jerry's, Walmart, Coca-Cola, Disney, Levi Strauss, and Toys 'R' Us are America. It is the precisely Americaness of these brands that makes them irresistible to so many—and despicable to so many."[94] America, the greatest merchant, has become the most prominent target. Corporate and government slowness in transforming Western living standards, so as the west expands we do not waste resources has only exacerbated this.

Chapter 6: Leading from the Front

In the midst of the challenges we face, leadership is the most dire challenge. We need leaders who can provide vision, purpose, and goals. Citizens, governments, and businesses require strategic vision and goals that will act like a lighthouse, providing beams of light so we can steer our way through the rocks of crisis. Human resource professionals who Top Grade[95] talent tell us only 25–40 percent of managers of companies that do not Top Grade are A players. An A player is defined as someone best in class. These numbers tell us that in politics and business, we have few excellent managers and leaders. We need leaders who will be able to work through conflict and drive fierce, crucial, and honest scientific and engineering-valid conversations with the public. This is a tough requirement, as Western society today, although still the leader in engineering, is more focused on legal solutions than engineering ones. The reality, however, is it is only by businesspeople and politicians working together with scientists, engineers, and supply chain professionals that changes can occur. Take the Rocky Mountain Institute, for example. Their work on reducing carbon footprints has had a tremendous impact across the United States and Canada. Their work has helped sell trailer skirts and transportation packages that reduce fuel consumption.

To achieve solutions, we will need to work though the conflict between conservatives, liberals, and the green movement that books such as *Climate Cover-Up*[96] detail from a green perspective and *Green Hell*[97] and *Red Hot Lies*[98] from a conservative perspective. This conflict between conservatives, liberals, and greens is confusing many, as the drop in the belief that there are issues to be addressed shows. This reduced concern is not good for any of us. Both sides pointing fingers at the other and making money from the issues and solutions will not stop the reality of what we are doing to the planet. This type of conflict is natural and required, as is political debate on the issues and the actions we need to take. However, such conflict and debate needs to be done in a way that clearly allows for progress. An industrial ecology board with independent public assessment of the details may help address this, but as business, government, and public leaders, we cannot wait for the completion of the debate or we will be waiting until the sun runs out of hydrogen.

One solution that would have supported our ability to measure the impact on the planet was America's Orbiting Carbon Observatory (OCO). The satellite that was intended for this role, however, was lost in 2009,[99] and until a network of monitoring stations called the Integrated Carbon Observation System is approved by the European Union, all measurements require detailed top-down or bottom-up work. The bottom-up approach uses data on activities and what each activity is expected to produce.

To guide our way through this as governments and corporations, we need leaders who will provide the resources to do the work needed. As pointed out before, both sides in the green discussion have a focus on making money.[100] Governments and business leaders also have a responsibility to mitigate integrity issues and can facilitate this duty by creating regulated or self-regulated approaches. An example of such a self-regulating approach is the Equator Principles (EPs), a voluntary set of standards to support responsible environmental stewardship and socially responsible development.[101] The statement of these principles is summarized below.

Summarized Principles

Statement of Principles

Principle 1: Review and Categorization
When a project is proposed for financing, the EPFI will, as part of its internal social and environmental review and due diligence, categorize each project based on the magnitude of its potential impacts and risks in accordance with the environmental and social screening criteria of the International Finance Corporation.

Principle 2: Social and Environmental Assessment
For each project assessed as being either Category A or Category B, the borrower conducts a social and environmental assessment ("assessment") process. The relevant social and environmental impacts and risks of the proposed project assessment should also propose mitigation and management measures relevant and appropriate to the nature and scale of the proposed project.

Principle 3: Applicable Social and Environmental Standards
Projects located in non-OECD countries, and for those located in OECD countries not designated as high-income, as defined by the World Bank Development Indicators Database, the assessment will establish to a participating EPFI's satisfaction the project's overall compliance with, or justified deviation from, the respective performance standards and EHS guidelines.

Principle 4: Action Plan and Management System
Borrowers will build on, maintain, or establish a social and environmental management system that addresses the management of the impacts, risks, and corrective actions required to comply with applicable host country social and environmental laws and regulations.

Principle 5: Consultation and Disclosure
For projects with significant adverse impacts on affected communities, the process will ensure their free, prior, and informed consultation and facilitate their informed participation as a means to establish, to the satisfaction of the EPFI, whether a project has adequately incorporated affected communities' concerns.

Principle 6: Grievance Mechanism
There is a mechanism for borrowers to receive and facilitate resolution of concerns and grievances about the project's social and environmental performance, as raised by individuals or groups from among project-affected communities. The borrower will inform the affected communities about the mechanism in the course of its community engagement process and ensure that the mechanism addresses concerns promptly and transparently in a culturally appropriate manner and is readily accessible to all segments of the affected communities.

Principle 7: Independent Review
For projects, an independent social or environmental expert not directly associated with the borrower will review the assessment, AP, and consultation process documentation in order to assist EPFIs' due diligence and assess Equator Principles compliance.

Principle 8: Covenants
Where a borrower is not in compliance with its social and environmental covenants, EPFIs will work with the borrower to bring it back into compliance to the extent feasible. If the borrower fails to reestablish compliance within an agreed-upon grace period, EPFIs reserve the right to exercise remedies as they consider appropriate.

Principle 9: Independent Monitoring and Reporting
To ensure ongoing monitoring and reporting over the life of the loan, EPFIs will, for all Category A projects and, as appropriate, for Category

B projects, require appointment of an independent environmental and/or social expert or require that the borrower retain qualified and experienced external experts to verify its monitoring information, which would be shared with EPFIs.

Principle 10: EPFI Reporting
Each EPFI adopting the Equator Principles commits to report publicly at least annually about its Equator Principles implementation processes and experience.

In the same way, Value Profit has core concepts, which are:

Core Concept 1: Leadership
Leadership needs to be based on honesty and truth in business, finances' life, and science. People, quality of life, and natural or environmental sustainability are the number-one asset and concern of Value Profit businesses.

Core Concept 2: Society must benefit
Business must benefit society while making a Value Profit and eliminating over time Easy Profits. Goals for Smart Profit Creation and Easy Profit Creation must be set.

Core Concept 3: Convert to Value Profits
Existing business practices driven by Easy Profits need to transfer to Value Profits for success. This transition is time based, as Value Profits today will turn to Easy Profits tomorrow as more companies attain that level of profitability and deplete resources further.

Core Concept 4: Shareholders and Customers must both benefit
Value Profits must benefit shareholders in the company, and products of the company must not hurt the ecology or their customers' physical health.

Core Concept 5: Value is promoted by planning and measurement
Value Profit businesses will create balanced scorecards incorporating cultural, social, and environmental measurements systems that include an assessment of these issues when decisions are made based on two, three, five, and ten-year plans.

Core Concept 6: Laws must be obeyed
Value Profit businesses will comply with all applicable country laws, social and environmental laws, and regulations.

Core Concept 7: Visibility
The company will ensure that its processes and procedures are clearly communicated and its intent is transparent so that the public is clear on the goals and objectives of the company.

Core Concept 8: Covenants
When a company adapts Vale Proof Processes, they will train their staff and develop their understanding of Easy versus Value Profits.

Leadership

Leaders are defined by many qualities, not just IQ and EOQ[102] but also by Ecological Intelligence,[103] which is a psychological way of defining our interaction as ecological leaders. Ecological intelligence fits directly into our Value Profitability message. Value Profitability is based on incorporating into our hearts the ideas and concepts that will make us leaders not only in our companies but in leading our companies' interactions with the world. Executives need to have a commitment to ecology, sustainability, and Value Profitability. You need to aim for Value Profits and plan your transition from Easy Profits. We need to emotionally crystallize the reality of our goal and use Value Profitability concepts like vitamins for the mind, building up the right framework and transforming our minds to the task.

To achieve profits today that will benefit you tomorrow will require leaders and managers who will lead by example. You may need to transition out existing staff to accomplish this. A focused, committed team is important, as a team needs a shared mindset of values and ideals. Leaders in the organization will need to be evangelists of a shared vision and goal, along with having the competence to deliver on objectives. Leadership is a quality and ability often discussed, yet it is one few people understand. The greatest leaders, to me, are servant leaders that demonstrate the characteristics of Jesus of Nazareth, a Jew respected by both Christians and Muslims. His leadership style, subsequently called Servant Leadership, demonstrated the ability to:

- ✓ Hold power lightly
- ✓ Give power away while still holding it
- ✓ Utilize judgment
- ✓ Communicate and live truth
- ✓ Trust others so trust could be learned
- ✓ Demonstrate in each situation the behavior he expected of others
- ✓ Never ask someone to do something he would not do himself
- ✓ Places others first
- ✓ Live and communicate the message he was given
- ✓ Respect his followers
- ✓ Embed commitment in his team
- ✓ Challenge people and situations when necessary
- ✓ Provide innovative new ideas
- ✓ Understand politics and its consequences but still make decisions based on what was best for family

The last point is critical, as leaders require a clear understanding of the importance of family. Our families are the future and the reason we are interested in Value Profit. Saving the world is nice, but if there is no one to share it with, that would be an empty victory.

The leader who moves a company to Value Profit or who leads in the new paradigm, whether it is Value Profit, Natural Capitalism, Factor Four or Ten, or any transformational role, does not have to be the head or the CEO. Indeed, transformation can come from inside the operation. The key to change really comes down to the same thing. To achieve change, a transformational management leader needs a team of committed, intelligent staff—people who can be trained and who will support their leader while he translates the goal into a vision for staff, stakeholders, members of the board, or CEOs. Your strategy for Value Profit or any of the ideas and concepts we discuss next, such as VBridge, must be dynamic and adjustable. As Carl von Clausewitz and Helmuth von Moltke wrote, "No plan survives contact with the enemy." This is as true in corporate life and ecology today as it is in war. This is why we need to trust the people we select as leaders and, more important, the followers who will participate in the business and government transformation we require. While principles can be abused, creating a covenant is a good starting place for a business culture to clarify its goals. Leaders are either challenged or constrained by the cultural goals that support them, so having a covenant of core principles is critical.

Chapter 7:
Organizational Transformation to Value Profits

An organizational transformation of the workforce needs to align with our leadership's mental and emotional transformation, crystallizing the new paradigm into the organizational DNA. Achieving this objective will require an ability to achieve cultural changes using vitamins for the mind and a focus on change management and transformation. Leaders will have to deal with many questions, such as:

- ✓ How do we communicate to our staff the new focus?
- ✓ What is the timeline?
- ✓ How do we encourage the hearts of the team while we change?
- ✓ How do we ensure it is not the flavor of the month?
- ✓ What tools will we have to support us in making the change?
- ✓ On what basis do we decide what to change and when?
- ✓ What toolkits are available to help us?
- ✓ Will we be allowed to change the team if needed?
- ✓ What is the financial impact of the change, and how do we measure success?

Above are the types of questions you will receive. To address them as managers and leaders, we will need to:

- ✓ Conduct a Business Health Assessment
- ✓ Access the organization's commitment and ability to implement
- ✓ Define leadership
- ✓ Set clear measurable goals
- ✓ Develop a Balanced Scorecard that incorporates the changes
- ✓ Align our plans with the scorecard across the organization and benchmark against other organizations
- ✓ Select an area for change
- ✓ Get finance to understand the concept
- ✓ Focus on small wins first, starting in supply chain and marketing
- ✓ Create a milestones chart
- ✓ Select a Steering Committee
- ✓ Select a team
- ✓ Develop the team
- ✓ Train the team
- ✓ Launch a project
- ✓ Measure success
- ✓ Adjust and expand the process

Becoming a profit organization means moving from theory to practice. To do this, you need to align the CEO, Finance, Human Resources, ISD, and Supply Chain heads behind the change and select a team lead who is dedicated to the concepts and processes. The team leader's role is to create a Center of Value Excellence whose goal is excellence, continuous improvement, and increased Value Profitability. Centers of Value Excellence will focus on:

- ✓ Customer Service Requirements
- ✓ Internal Customer interface and collaboration
- ✓ External Communication

- ✓ Continuous Improvement
- ✓ Value Profit leadership
- ✓ Cost leadership

Centers of Value Excellence need to arise across the business, starting with the first one. The Center of Value Excellence Team needs to demonstrate:

- ✓ Shared goals
- ✓ Commitment
- ✓ Teamwork
- ✓ Fun
- ✓ Communication
- ✓ Concern for others
- ✓ Involve staff in decision
- ✓ Being a change agent

Senior leadership is a substantial investment for any company in a project, yet having this level of leadership is integral to growing and nurturing the changes required for a Value Profit culture. Investment in people is also critical. An example of the benefits of investment in people was demonstrated during my time at Unilever, where our division invested in the staff and the people. The comradeship, relationships, and excellence developed there lasted for years, and our team still supports each other although we are years and often miles away in different companies. The investment in the staff nourished an environment of success and continuity. To move to a Value Profit company culture and leadership, we need to ask ourselves questions such as:

Do I have the desire to look after my children, providing a place that they can live healthy, productive lives?

Today I just found out that my father has cancer, the same cancer my grandfather had. I do not blame the cancer on pollution, as both my grandfather and my dad were diagnosed at the same age. Instead, it appears my family has a genetic predisposition. In my case, my options to address my potential for cancer are limited to increased testing, exercising, losing weight, and eating better. I am determined to do all those things. In the case of the planet, we face similar choices to improve it or to continue existing behavior. My choice is to improve it for my family if God grants us the time. The things I can do include writing this book, teaching my wife and daughters about the environment, which I have been doing, and leading the way. I need and want to grant our daughters the best possible place to live, and so should you. However, we need to do so without using fear as a motivator..

Scaring children with the fear that the planet will soon die is not the way to go. While we need to educate consumers and workers in how to look after the planet, we need to ensure we are not building fear into our children. I remember very well as a six to nine-year-old discussing nuclear war, surviving fallout, and the fear that every time a jet went overhead it might be a missile. Training that motivates change based on fear should not be an option. Instead, we need to focus on what we can do to transform the world, as based on our responsibility to our children to provide and care for them.

Do I have a desire to improve my company's value for the future?

Striving for value has a motivation, a cache all its own. When I think of value and motivation to improve, the Toyota saying comes to mind: "Best is not a destination, best is a way." This may sound corny, but the statement is correct—best is not a destination. We can always improve our people, processes, and profits. If we are motivated to achieve higher numbers, we will develop plans and processes to do so. If we are motivated to look at our business from a value perspective and drive for improvement, we will look and develop the tools to look at the total input cost of our products and develop products that will make a difference. Some authors tear apart changes the green movement has suggested, such as smaller cars, fuel-efficient cars, and identifying that accidents have increased for smaller cars. However, the problem, if you look at the move to smaller cars, is not the car size but that we have not developed a transition plan to develop safe, ultra-lightweight, fuel-efficient cars while exiting away from heavy, steel-bodied fuel users. The leaders of Rocky Mountain Institute noted in their book, *Natural Capitalism*, that:

> Weight is not a prerequisite for strength. Today's advanced composite materials make this especially true: Crash tests have proven that innovative ultra-light designs are at least as safe as standard cars, even in high-speed collisions with bridge abutments or with heavy steel vehicles. Composites are so extraordinary strong that they can absorb five times more energy per pound than steel. About ten pounds of hollow, crushable carbon fiber and plastics cones can smoothly absorb the entire crash energy of a 1,300-pound car hitting a wall at 50 mph.[104]

Assuming what we have today is the best we can achieve is part of the problem, causing people to no longer look for innovation and change. However, workers in the West, with their access to information and their freedom to leverage their imaginations for ideas and concepts, can transform the costs of an organization if given the freedom to think, collaborate, and act with their cousins in engineering overseas. So let's start with the basics of how you can transform your business with Value Profitability.

Business Health Assessment

So, how does your business start the move to Value Profit? The place to start is with what we call a Business Health Assessment. It is recommended that you get an outside resource to do the assessment below, as a different perspective on the opportunities in your business will provide additional value to you.

Business Health Assessment

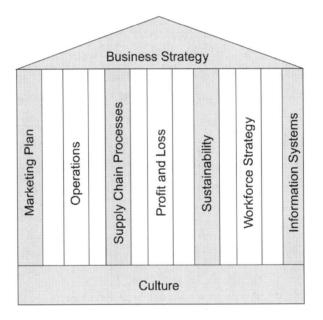

Table 10

The Business Health Assessment is an analysis of:

- ✓ Culture
- ✓ Business Strategy
- ✓ Profit and Loss
- ✓ Marketing strategy
- ✓ Manufacturing or vendor management

- ✓ Supply Chain processes
- ✓ Sustainability initiatives and assessment
- ✓ Workforce strategy
- ✓ Information systems technology

Culture

If profit is the lifeblood of an organization, its culture is the heart, transporting the blood to nourish the organizational tissues. Cultures exist in the minds and hearts of people. They affect our actions and are the core of a corporation's personality. The reason I use the word personality here is that corporations, along with a few other virtual entities, are legal non-persons that you can take to court.

Table 11

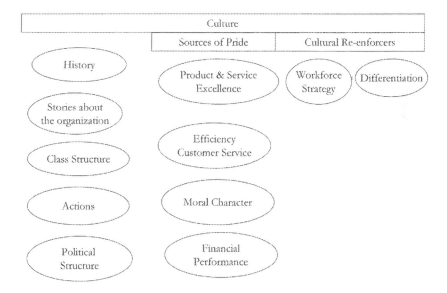

Assessing your business culture is important, as it allows you to see with a cultural review:

✓ How your culture is perceived internally and externally?

✓ What your culture says ?

✓ What your culture does ?

✓ Its effectiveness

✓ Its ability to grow

✓ How it aligns with your workforce strategy?

✓ How it will accept a change to Value Profitability?

Culture depends on companies and staff having mutual goals. Toyota[105] believes that mutual prosperity creates partnership. However, from our experience, mutual goals build trust based on long-term prosperity. Below is a chart showing how mutual goals and trust are supported by long-term prosperity. You can see this in your own company where as the Great Recession bit in, the trust between associates and the company decreased as layoffs and terminations increased.

Table 12

Mutual Goals

Company Goals
• Profit
• Long Term Success
• Contribute to the Economy
• Contribute to Society
• Excellent Quality
• Environmental Management

Trust

Employee Goals
• Paycheck
• Growth
• Group Benefits
• Safe Workplace
• Interesting Work
• Meaningful work

Long Term Prosperity

However, long-term prosperity cannot be achieved without factoring in the government and persevering the environment. An alternative view including the environment is shown next. As you can see, government has a larger role to play than business and must address the population in at least two ways—as citizens and as employees. Business also has an interaction with government, and that interaction includes dependencies on the government's management of resources for long-term prosperity. The culture of a business is therefore key, as it affects not only a corporation's interactions with employees but also with the government, which has taken on a larger role in corporate life for many companies since the Great Recession began. Even if your company has minimal interaction with the government, including this aspect into a cultural assessment is important.

Table 13

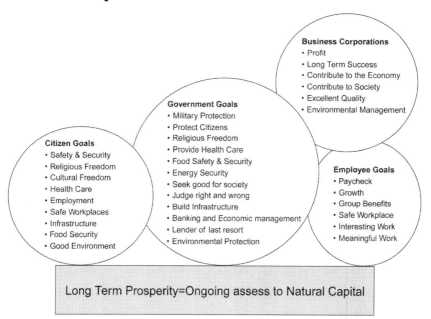

Expanded Mutual Goals

All of the above points are important if you are to understand your culture and incorporate into it a new message regarding Easy Profits, Natural Capital, and Value Profits. While this may appear to be a straightforward message, it is a crucial financial and marketing message in a situation where even small cultural items matter. For example, in China, yelling and banging on the table and dressing inappropriately sends a message that you are a barbarian and causes foreigners to lose face. Having dinner can be a trial in different cultures, as Germans may want to concentrate on their meal and not converse too much, while an Italian may want to talk during the meal. Just because everyone in our business speaks the same language, we should not assume they have the same understanding and will accept a change easily.

Cultures can be very different from each other, even in the same company. For example, the culture I experienced in Unilever U.S. was different from the culture in Unilever Canada and from Unilever in Rotterdam. In some European companies, for example, you can drink at work and the atmosphere is much less frantic. In Canada and the United States, there is no drinking at work. Culture in a business is critical and is one of the key reasons that mergers and acquisitions fail or succeed and business changes work or fail. We must not expect messages to be transferred, absorbed, and crystallized into a culture unless we translate them into messages and stories the culture can understand. The culture of a company includes items such as:

- ✓ Non-oral communication, such as office placement
- ✓ Who has an office versus who has a cube
- ✓ Is there an open door policy
- ✓ Is there a cultural policy
- ✓ Are people friendly
- ✓ Is the company highly political or moderately political
- ✓ What are the traditions and the degree to which the established order is emphasized
- ✓ The history of the corporation
- ✓ Food and eating behavior
- ✓ Corporate class structure
- ✓ Rate of technological and social change

- ✓ Organization and perspective on work ethic
- ✓ How minorities are treated

To introduce Value Profits into a culture it is not enough for the executive suite to buy into it. We have to also:

- ✓ Explain the message.
- ✓ Contextualize the new message within the culture.
- ✓ Create expectations for how members of the corporation will act when given the new message.
- ✓ Understand what members of the government, public, and corporation assume about the relationship between staff, nature, and the corporation. That is, should we live in harmony with it or subjugate it? Do we exploit it for our profit or are we stewards of natural capital?
- ✓ Explain value and allow value debates and challenges. Should these be public or held in private?
- ✓ Identify if everyone participates in meetings and decision making, whether we allow emotions to be expressed publicly about the change.
- ✓ Detail the corporation's or government's timeline for change.

All of these items need to be considered to make the change work and stick. As we work on making the cultural adaptation to Value Profitability, we will need to look at the morale in the company and evaluate the impact the changes are having. A key part of a company's employee enthusiasm is the pride employees have in the company. In *The Enthusiastic Employee*,[106] the authors, based on their research, identify that there is a:

> "Strong correlation between pride in an organization and the overall satisfaction of workers with that organization. We find that there are four main sources of pride, all of which reflect different facets of a single attribute-excellence:

✓ Excellence in the organization's financial performance
✓ Excellence in the efficiency with which the work of the organization is done
✓ Excellence in the characteristics of the organization's products such as their usefulness, distinctiveness, and quality
✓ Excellence in the organization's moral character

People want to work for an organization that does well but also does good."

It is in this context that the authors make the comment that "employees want their companies to do very well and a lot of good."[107] This is important when it comes to the message of Value Profit, as Value Profit facilitates companies doing all four of the key items that are good for employee pride:

✓ Increasing financial performance over time
✓ Increasing efficiency
✓ Focusing on improving the characteristics of the company's products
✓ Creating excellence in the organization's moral character

A key step in changing your culture is adding Value Profitability into your Workforce Strategy[108] as one of the items of differentiation. Adding Value Profit to your Workforce Strategy enables you to hold staff accountable for implementing new processes and the changes in the organizational culture required.

An example of this is an organization in which the department I was responsible for had significant responsibility but no ability to change things, as they had allowed their third-party providers to gain power and control over them. To achieve change, we needed to change the paradigm from one where my managers lacked power and ability and, my team's decisions were an after thought. We needed a new paradigm in which the third parties saw us as the decision makers and came to us for decisions. This was a radial transformation. To make this transition, a strategy that would deliver millions in savings, needed to be crafted, and messages had to be delivered to both the executive and the staff on the potential upside. We had to shape their thoughts over time so that the executive gained confidence in our abilities to deliver millions in savings and service and the staff gained the knowledge and ability to make the appropriate decisions. This was not an easy transition.

In the end, only strategy, tactics with expertise, knowledge and confidence, and detailed analysis (and prayer) allowed delivery. Key to this was the realization that the external perspective of the company and the internal message from other areas were ones of excellence and ability. Transferring that perception to the team aided us in making the change and moving the needle with the third party. We had some really fierce conversations, but within eighteen months, the transformation was complete and the savings were achieved.

These changes and savings were based on applying the same principles that are shown, taking a new message, and adding it into the mix. In the above case, there was an interim step of sales, as you need to *sell* the message to the executive to have it incorporated and *sell* the message to line staff to have them believe it. This requires working across boundaries and political obstacles and translating the concept into the ideas and needs of the business. In this case, the need of the business was profit. However, in every case that I have seen this work effectively on a large scale, it has been for profit, which is what we are aiming for—just not Easy Profit, but Value Profit.

This is why the Business Health Assessment is important. It acts like an antibody, taking in foreign material and engineering material to aid you in developing the right strategy to address the issues your company faces. An example of utilizing an early version of the Business Health

Assessment is when I was sent to England to review closing an assembly plant. The product the plant made was important, as not only was it the moneymaker for the company, but also it was a historical legacy of the organization—the company was built on sales of this product. In the same way we would do a Business Health Assessment, I did one for the company in the form of a report. The report identified to the presidents that while we could save some money closing the plant, it would have a negative workforce impact in a time when the business had brand-new leadership, the staff had already been studied to death on closing the plant, and the process had been redesigned two to three times. In summary, the profit impact would be outweighed by what it did to an organization in the midst of turmoil. The answer in every case in business is to not make Easy Profits but make the decisions that make Value Profits for the company. In some cases, this may mean putting money into a loss leader, as the loss leader may have a significant impact on the company in ways that cannot be measured by profit. Some things need to be measured by cultural loss.

Table 14

Cultural Transformation

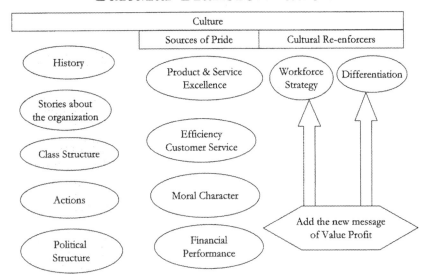

Table 15 is a chart showing a leader-driven business change model. This type of leader-driven change process is driven by an external issue affecting the organization. This is important as we are discussing cultural change, and we will need a leader to drive the change. External issues such as profit, mergers, and market adjustments, or even internal issues, can drive the need for change. The more difficult the challenge, the more pressure is applied to change. Stresses are put on leadership to select a direction. The new direction affects the people, and the change is used to try to create a new culture. This type of model is often where you have a political environment with little true bottom-up communication. In a case such as this, the leader might select change and drive the change in the business. However, if the leader leaves and the message has not been incorporated into the company DNA, very quickly the message will dissipate.

Table 15

Leader Driven Business Change Model

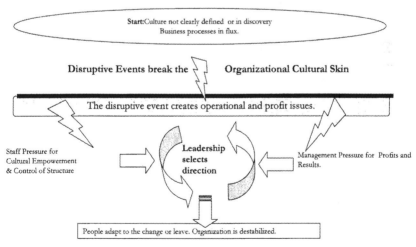

Major change drivers: Economic, Low Sales, Innovation, Customers issues, systems, merger or lack of profit.

Alternatively, change can be servant leader driven as in table 16. In a servant leader-driven culture, the leader works with the existing culture of the organization to balance it. The leader is dedicated to balancing change, empowerment, and structure. In this situation, the culture and leadership work in harmonic tension, and ideas can come from both the leadership and the staff. Once the ideas are brought to the leader and the business, the transformation is faster and more efficient.

Table 16
Servant Leader Driven Business Change Model

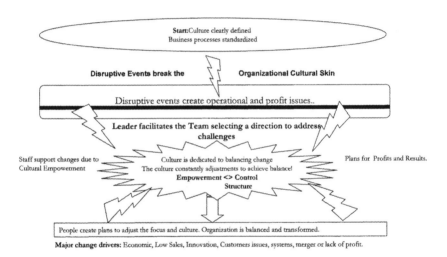

In both cases, a transformation can take place. However, it is more effective and lasting in the servant leader driven model. Especially as optimization should not be dependent on the leader.

Business Strategy

Today we are just starting to come out of the Great Recession, and we face significant change ahead. Looking back at past recessions, as David Rhodes and Daniel Stelter have done in *Accelerating Out of the Great Recession*, can provide some strategies for addressing the future. However, many of these strategies are based on not factoring in the key variables of business trends we face. Examples of what can be done that their historical review provides include:

- ✓ Protecting financial fundamentals
- ✓ Protecting business fundamentals
- ✓ Protecting revenue[109]

These are all good steps, and we need to take them as they align with Value Profitability and addressing costs for reinvestment. However, we also need to move beyond that and look at the basic strategies we are utilizing. For an excellent walkthrough of corporate strategy, read *Strategy Safari*.[110] The book takes you through all the different types of strategic schools:

- ✓ Strategy as a Formal Process
- ✓ Strategy as a Visionary Process
- ✓ Strategy as a Mental Process
- ✓ Strategy as a process of transformation

There are many strategic processes, but what we need to focus on is strategy as a method of making profit within the context of your country, society, culture, and P&L opportunities and limitations. You need to look at the integrated strategic model that you have created for your business and assess if that model is working for you in coordination and collaboration with the other facets of your business. Together, we need to examine your strategy and see if it is addressing the standard processes via a SWOT analysis. However, you should also look at your strategy within the context of Michael Porter's positioning schools' three generic strategic approaches.[111]

Overall cost leadership, where a company takes the low-cost position and via aggressive use of efficiency, scale, and management of costs, seizes the low-cost leader position, which is hard for other companies to defend against. This position also provides barriers to entry. An example of a company that exemplifies low-cost leader ship today is Walmart, as it has the scale, market share, and operations in the low price range, allowing for economies of scale and an exacting example of what Porter describes.

Differentiation, Porter's second strategy, is based on differentiating the product and services by creating a unique product. Porter describes differentiation as a viable strategy for earning above-average returns in an industry because it creates a defensible position for coping with the five competitive forces. Differentiation, however, may prevent you from gaining a higher market share.

Focus is about selecting a target market, segment of a line, or geographic market. The strategy is based on the company serving its market more effectively and efficiently than its competitors.[112]

Today, we have mix-and-match strategies that come into play because of market and business leadership changes resulting from technology that has opened up different options. Look at the transformation of IBM from a maker of equipment to a company where a significant part of the revenue comes from software (40 percent) and from consulting work (42 percent).[113] Alternatively, Dell was based on differentiation and cost. In my opinion, we need to add to the positioning school three additional strategic options.

Global resource utilization needs to be added as a strategy because it relates to the methods, processes, and strategies we take to utilize the natural capital resources that we have available.

Technology via email, websites, and blogs has now impacted and altered strategy in so many ways that it needs to be considered as another strategic path.

Value leadership is where companies take the value position and via use of efficiency, scale, cost control, and a management of quality and resource management, seize the Value leader position, which is hard for other companies to defend against. This position also provides barriers to entry. An example of a company that exemplified Value leadership was Toyota, as it had the quality, and it offered customers perceived high value, scale, market share, and operations in a higher price range while still allowing for economies of scale using innovation.

The Business Health Assessment reviews how your business fits within these six strategies, and it evaluates your internal abilities and external competition.

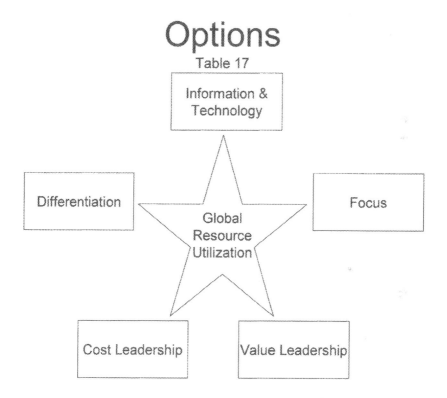

Options
Table 17

Information & Technology

Differentiation

Global Resource Utilization

Focus

Cost Leadership

Value Leadership

Strategic Alignment

To assess your business strategy, you need to look at the above six areas, then, in conjunction with your marketing strategy, evaluate your company's brand and value position and what changes need to take place to drive transformation. You also need to review your customer and workforce strategy alignment, as we discussed earlier. Having a Balanced Scorecard aligned with your strategy will support optimal tactical implementation. To summarize, the key barriers to strategic success that Kaplan and Notion identify[114] are:

- ✓ Vision and strategy are not actionable, usually due to the organization's inability to translate vision and strategy into actionable steps.
- ✓ Strategy is not linked to departmental team and individual goals.
- ✓ Strategy is not linked to resource allocation
- ✓ Feedback is tactical, not strategic, so you cannot see whether the strategy is being implemented and working.

Once your business strategy is understood, you need to review your P&L. Also, see how Easy Profits and Value Profits are integrated into your P&L.

P&L

A P&L is critical in making the right decisions on culture, branding, and the message you provide as you change your company around. As a corporation or a partnership, each business has stakeholders that we need to sell on the changes that we are making, and the easy way to make this sell is by looking at and finding ways to improve your P&L. To start with, you need to understand:

- ✓ How your P&L is structured
- ✓ What your P&L says about your business
- ✓ What your P&L is used for and does for you
- ✓ Its effectiveness
- ✓ Its ability to grow
- ✓ If it aligns with your business strategy
- ✓ If it can be divided into Easy Profits & Value Profits

A P&L is like a report card for a business. It gives us a measured assessment of how well a company is doing. Numbers can be deceptive, as we all know. However, if we understand how the P&L is designed and put together, we can understand the key drivers and levers in a business. In one business, every P&L I saw for months was a disaster. In this business, the numbers were so badly put together that we had swings of a million dollars at the end of each week. We constantly had to provide explanations and be up late at night, reviewing and trying to adjust the numbers because the finance system was a disaster. P&Ls are like a mirror for the company. In this case, they could not get the P&L to work, and in less than a year they went through two controllers and an assistant controller, and the numbers were still a struggle. In a company like that, understanding the P&L requires extensive work. Unfortunately, companies such as this are not rare. This is why it is critical to do an assessment of your P&L. The assessment is to help you understand both what your existing P&L can tell you and what your existing P&L cannot tell you.

P&L management is of critical importance, as management, marketing, operations, supply chain, stakeholders, and shareholders get information on the flow of the blood from the P&L. Imagine going in for an operation and the doctor or nurse neglects to check your blood pressure. You could be bleeding internally, and no one would know until you were dead. It is the same with a company. Your P&L provides critical information to the business.

Now, some companies look at their P&Ls monthly, and some weekly. This is insufficient to keep a patient healthy. Great companies, like great doctors and nurses, will check a patient daily, sometimes more than once a day. In the same way, in a hospital there is a trade-off between staff costs and patient health. In the case of a P&L, there is a trade-off between frequency and costs of preparation. Two of the best companies I have seen check their P&Ls daily and weekly. This is done by creating financial forecasts of sales and costs daily in an abbreviated format. The full P&L is then reviewed weekly with managers, and monthly with the management team. However, flash or other reports are needed daily.

Firstly, "flash" or daily forecasts are needed by the business in the morning. The daily numbers tell management where they are, if they need to react to issues, and if steps are being taken to address losses in sales and operations. If there are major changes from day to day, the reports show them and also how far the business is from achieving its sales goals so that actions can be taken. It is the same as if the nurse called a specialist or a doctor based on your blood pressure and results. A CEO, CMO, and CSO (chief supply-chain officer) can react based on these reports. The key thing in this case is that the numbers need to be sliced in different ways for the different needs of the business. An overall business report will not help the CSO, and so he needs a specific report designed for this purpose.

The marketing, merchandising, and supply chain departments will require different P&L formats. These reports will tell the business areas how effective they have been and identify risks to operating fundamentals. These forecasts, or flash reports, will tell people the benefits and risks if sales go up and down. During times of vulnerability, this information is critical to the decision-making process. Without this information, the patient will either get sicker or die. Identifying risk also means that we need explanations and solutions to problems. These assessments need to be done quickly and modeled so that alternatives can be assessed and decisions made. To support this, a company's analytics department needs staff who can not only use the existing tools that come with SAP, Oracle, or other ERP systems, but Excel as well, as in many cases Excel allows for analysis of the data in different ways and formats. A P&L requires inputs that are:

- ✓ Accurate
- ✓ Timely
- ✓ ABC costed
- ✓ Standardized

The P&L must show data on:

- ✓ Costs
- ✓ Purchases
- ✓ POS sales
- ✓ Raw material needs
- ✓ Product or service mix
- ✓ Labor
- ✓ Value
- ✓ Origin and destination
- ✓ Transportation costs
- ✓ Transportation shipments
- ✓ Warehousing costs
- ✓ Productivity
- ✓ R&D
- ✓ Disposal costs
- ✓ Cost to design for the Environment
- ✓ Cost to design for disassembly

These inputs are all needed to carry out the assessment. Specific cutoffs need to be applied to ensure the data is current and real time. Errors to avoid in the data include late production and sales data, incorrectly formatted date, or linked data. To interpret a P&L, you need to understand the business so you can interpret the data in a meaningful way. Table 18, below, is a grid of other reports and characteristics areas in your business you should review:

Below are sample P&L categories to give you an idea of the way data can be looked at and reviewed by area.

TABLE 18		
Operations	Supply Chain	Logistics
Sales	Sales	Sales
Rate of Sales	Rate of Sales	Rate of Sales
Employee Turnover	Employee Turnover	Employee Turnover
Wages	Wages	Wages
Training	Training	Training
Cost per case	Rate of Sales	Cases per hr
Cases per hr	Cases per hr	Costs per DC
Maintenance	Fill rate by vendor	Fill rate
Work in Process	Forecast Accuracy	On time in Full
Waste	Inventory turns	Outbound cases per truck
Downtime	Inventory turns per planner	Inbound costs
Finished Inventory	On hand inventory	Fuel costs
Cycle Time	WIP	Lease costs
Set-up costs	Raw material Inventory	Warehouse receipts in cases
House Keeping	Finished Goods Inventory	Cases shipped by DC
Insurance	Lead time	Maintenance
Average case value	Item File Accuracy	House Keeping
Environmental Proofing	Average case value	Average case value
	Environmental Proofing	Environmental Proofing
	Order size	Shipping Accuracy
	Store days on hand	Picking Accuracy

In Table 19, below, are sample P&L categories to give you an idea of the way to look at and reviewed data by area.

Marketing	Merchandising	Human Resources	Store Operations
Market Share	Sales	Sales	Sales
Rate of Sales	Rate of Sales	Rate of Sales	Rate of Sales
Employee Turnover	Employee Turnover	Employee Turnover	Employee Turnover
Training	Wages	Hiring	Sales per sq ft
Sales	Training	Wages	Sales by Department
Rate of Sales	Fill rate by Vendor	Training	Sales by Region
Wages	Size of basket	House Keeping	Sales by Store type
Customer Service	Market downs	Employee surveys	Sales per Customer
TV Advertising	Average case value	Performance Evaluations	Size of basket
Admail	Sales per sq ft	Benefits	Wages
Agency	Profits per case	Applicants Interviews	Training
Average case value	Coop costs	Cultural activities	Logistics cost per Region
Environmental Proofing	Environmental Proofing	Environmental Proofing	Environmental Proofing
			Maintenance
			Waste
			Sales per employee
			House Keeping
			Average case value

Below, in Table 20, is a more detailed operational P&L example.

TABLE 20				
Manufacturing	Plant 1	Ratio to Sales	Plant 2	Ratio to Sales
Sales ($) by Plant				
Sales by cases by plant				
Production Hours used				
Productive Hours				
Unproductive				
Line 1 cases				
Line 1 Capacity				
Line 1 Cost				
Line 2 cases				
Line 2 Capacity				
Line 2 Cost				
Line 3 cases				
Line 3 Capacity				
Line 3 Cost				
Management				
Hourly staff				
Storage				
Utilities				
Vacation				
Lost time Accidents				
Material used				
Inventory Costs				
Scrap written off				
Quality Issues				
Defect PPM				
Defectives PPM				
Disposal costs				
Environmental Proofing				
Total Cost				

These detailed P&Ls need to be reviewed weekly and monthly, and flash versions of them daily. During the Business Health Assessment, key items that will need review include:

- ✓ Profitability
- ✓ Inventory levels
- ✓ Sales vs. inventory levels in days inventory on hand
- ✓ Quality issues
- ✓ Methods of gathering the data
- ✓ What the data is used for
- ✓ If you are fixing issues before they take place
- ✓ The speed you are getting the information

✓ Who is reviewing the P&L
✓ Accuracy of the sales for the last three months to the achieved results

A Business Health Assessment must review each area's P&L results, your corporate business strategy, and alignment with the marketing plan.

Marketing Plans

The marketing assessment reviews your existing marketing plans and their alignment with culture, strategy, P&L goals, and results to validate that the approach is working. Marketing starts with a brand message and a brand position. The marketing department needs to be involved in the development of the business approach to Value Profitability. Brands are assets, as you can see by the value placed on some of the more value brands in the world, such as:

Coca-Cola
FedEx
Target
Tesco
Walmart

Customers interpret products based on both price and brand positioning. A brand is a visual, graphic representation of a company's historical achievements and future expectations, both positive and negative. People interpret product value and cost benefit based on the brand. Brands can be images like Apple, words like Coca-Cola, or a name like IBM. The reason the Business Health Assessment reviews marketing is to understand what the brand position has been, will be, and what it represents to consumers. If a brand represents low-cost, low-value items, trying to change that brand into a more valuable asset will be very difficult, and a Value Profit strategy may require repositioning or creating a new brand to represent the higher position and move customers upstream to a different brand position and value. Brands are the value tags of consumerism. People know that Tommy Hilfiger has a certain value versus another brand. Your brand is the primary marketing communication tool for your company's position in the marketplace. You need to ensure that your brand is enhanced by your move to Value Profitability as customers learn the benefits and the commitment your company has made to the future of their children.

In some organizations, such as retail and manufacturing, marketing has additional major components, which may be a part of marketing or separate areas:

- ✓ Merchandising, which consists of the merchant-selection team that decides on what items to buy.
- ✓ Product Development, which designs products.

All Marketing costs including Return on Marketing Investment need to be assessed.

Manufacturing and Vendor Management

In the Business Health Assessment, manufacturing is separate from supply chain. Having worked in automotive, food, consumer packaged goods, and even heavy equipment manufacturing, I have an appreciation for the intricacies and differences that can occur between different types of manufacturing. Yet, at the same time that each operation is different, many have the same characteristics. You can tell a well-run operation within hours of watching the staff and speaking with the managers. Failure has a scent all its own, as does success.

A key fact of manufacturing is variance. It is process variability that a Business Health Assessment reviews, and the operations that drive that variability allows you to understand and see what is affecting your success. Raw material inventory, inventory turns, and improper application of Best Practice techniques tell you many things about an organization. As manufacturing is such a critical focus, the purpose of the health check is not to define what you are doing wrong or right but to provide a summary of the overall operation. To understand operations from an executive approach, read *Velocity*,[115] an excellent book on operations management in a novel form.

In the Business Health Assessment, we will evaluate your overall performance to objectives and the KPIs that have been set.

Key items to review will include:

- ✓ Quality Assurance and Quality Control
- ✓ Demand Forecasting and Mean Absolute Error
- ✓ Supplier control
- ✓ Layout
- ✓ Performance appraisals
- ✓ Motivation and leadership
- ✓ Equipment dependability and maintenance
- ✓ Space utilization and functional layout
- ✓ 5S use
- ✓ Inventory planning
- ✓ Product flow
- ✓ Coordination between the DC and the plant
- ✓ Orders shipped on time
- ✓ Material arriving on time
- ✓ Case fill
- ✓ Rework/scrap
- ✓ Workforce flexibility

The Business Health Assessment will confirm if there is a need for the application of other tools such as:

- ✓ Lean Manufacturing

✓ Six Sigma
✓ Theory of Constraints

Supply Chain Processes

Supply Chain in the Business Health Assessment covers off the following:

✓ Item File
✓ Modular/Plannogram Planning
✓ Demand and Independent Demand Forecasting
✓ Material planning
✓ Material management
✓ Bill of Materials
✓ Inventory management
✓ Distribution Requirement Planning
✓ Replenishment
✓ Fulfillment
✓ Third- Party management
✓ Buying and procurement

Logistics

✓ Customer service
✓ Product flow
✓ Inbound transportation
✓ Outbound transportation
✓ Warehousing
✓ Warehouse inventory
✓ Pallet control

Supply Chain Planning and Logistics are closely related to each other, with logistics in some organizations subordinate to supply chain. Supply Chain consists of the material planning, command, and control processes for business items. In addition, all buying and vendor management functions need to reside in a central purchasing organization that reports into the supply chain. Logistics consists of the physical storage and distribution of products and services in workplaces and facilities, nationally or globally. The Business Health Assessment will assess standard operating processes for each area and their effectiveness. Supply Chain and Logistics staff need the ability to understand the overall process integration of their areas but also their impact and to have the analytical ability to use the tools and systems provided. Without the correct training and processes, Supply Chains and Logistics systems can operate but will be sub-optimized, as they need to function together, not separately.

Information Systems and Technology

Information systems and their use today are important to operational efficiency. SAP, Oracle, Manugistics, and other ERP systems, modular or proprietary, are integral to the distribution and management of data for businesses and government to ensure that the correct information can be assessed and decisions made. Systems tie organizations together and ensure that communication is taking place and data processed in MRP, Customer systems such as Sales and Demand Management. If the systems are sub-optimized, the enterprise is sub-optimized. Systems are an enabler to all prior and subsequent processes. In assessing, we need to review:

- ✓ Documentation
- ✓ Operational requirements
- ✓ Information needs
- ✓ Integration
- ✓ System capability
- ✓ Data integrity
- ✓ Functionality

✓ EDI use
✓ Training
✓ Current requirements
✓ Future requirements

Sustainability Initiatives and Assessment

A sustainability assessment identifies how well an organization has incorporated environmental intelligence into its DNA, business plans and areas of focus to leverage its knowledge to improve sustainable processes and reduce environmental costs.

Example of a Sustainability Assessment	TABLE 21 Priority	Spend	Rating
Culture	A	B	AXB
Environmental Proofing			
Marketing Approach			
Manufacturing			
Supply Chain Processes			
Warehousing			
Warehouse Building			
Transportation			
Utilities			
Equipment			
Manufacturing Process			
Manufacturing Site			
Workforce Strategy			
Community Service			
Waste Usage			
Disposal			
Disassembly			
Material Recycling			
Carbon Footprint			
Water Usage			
Ocean Impact			
Energy Utilization			
Type of Energy			
Land Impact			
Life Cycle Product impact			
Vendor Processes			
Buying Processes			

A sustainability assessment allows us to see if your organization understands the cost benefits of different options and utilizes the appropriate options when called for. For example, does your logistics department know that ocean shipping is seventeen times more fuel efficient than air and ten times more efficient than road per container moved? Does your transportation team:

- ✓ Have a backhaul program?
- ✓ Review origin and destination pairs?
- ✓ Utilize consolidated shipping for LTL?
- ✓ Utilize routing software to optimize shipping?
- ✓ Use container transloading, street turns, and other strategies to cut inland fuel costs?[116]

Table 22

Energy Use by Type of Vehicle

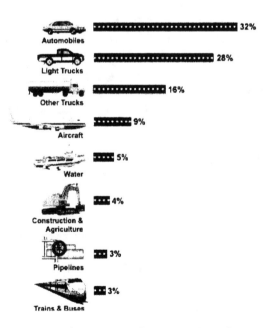

Source: National Energy Education Development Project

Workforce Strategy

A Workforce Strategy was covered in the earlier section on culture, as a Workforce Strategy looks at the incorporation of business goals into the business process to ensure that the Workforce Strategy fulfills the business strategy. This assessment looks at Human Resource processes and procedures, including:

- ✓ Clarity of cultural values
- ✓ Employee understanding of goals
- ✓ Employee empowerment to make decisions
- ✓ Understanding of the business strategy within the organization
- ✓ Staff competence
- ✓ Understanding of the Workforce Strategy

Business Health Assessment

Once you have completed a Business Health Assessment, you are ready to review alternative business models to allow for Strategic Flexibility. In addition to Strategic Flexibility, we need tactical and operational flexibility to ensure complete integration of all business functions and operational alignment of the business once a strategy is agreed upon. This integration must be across culture, strategy, marketing, finance, manufacturing, supply chain, logistics, and information technology. This process, which we call Integrated Value Chain Management, or VBridge, is what we will review in the next chapter.

Chapter 8:
A VBridge to Sustainable Profitability

Business strategic and tactical flexibility and expertise are required to address the multiple problems we face today. We need to develop multiple options, so as the world changes we have the flexibility to adjust in business and in government. In the 21st century, businesses continue the battle for optimized supply chains and logistics. Retail, manufacturing, health, and governments view value chains and supply chains as strategic cornerstones. Along with sales and marketing, supply chain and logistics areas are no longer just about material and inventory, transportation and warehousing. Supply chains have taken over activities such as purchasing and quality. A supply chain, however, is a part of a greater whole called the value chain, which extends backwards into product design and product selection and forward into retail store design from backroom to sales floor, all the way to the store cash register. Unfortunately, supply chains in many companies are often not integrated with other value chain sub-components. While sales and operations planning proponents have attempted this coordination, most companies struggle to make coordination a success. This is where Value Chain Integrated Management, or VBridge, comes into effect. A VBridge approach integrates Value Chain processes from product design to customer satisfaction management. From discontinuation to the integrated continuous flow of the intellectual capital, operating processes, and systematic computerized systems covering product design, supply chain and customers product use.

In a VBridge, business strategy links with branding and merchandising strategy, supporting marketing and the operations strategy. In the middle, linking the strategic elements is the VBridge, which links all of the pieces together operationally via extending supply chain and logistics processes across the organization so that the ten planks of the VBridge act as stepping stones for efficiency. Four of those planks are adjusted versions of the V4L Learning Principle of Toyota, and the other six are integral components of Value Profitability.

VBridge Integration Change

Egg Shell Theory
- Equal pressure on all surfaces of an egg prevents collapse.
- Leaders have time to manage change and develop value.

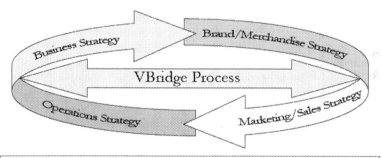

Link the organization like an egg shell and apply pressure equally
Use the VBridge to nurture internal changes while keeping the outside strong.

Table 23

In today's fragmented business, a siloed department is normal but highly dysfunctional, as it will allow:

✓ Inventory to increase as the systems for buying are not integrated with the company system for marketing

- ✓ Warehouse space to increase
- ✓ Transportation costs to increase
- ✓ Vendors to lack specification information
- ✓ Redeliveries not to be coordinated or collaborative
- ✓ Products not to meet extra specifications
- ✓ Easy Profits to be the objective
- ✓ Environmental impacts not to be considered

Table 24

Today's Fragmented Business

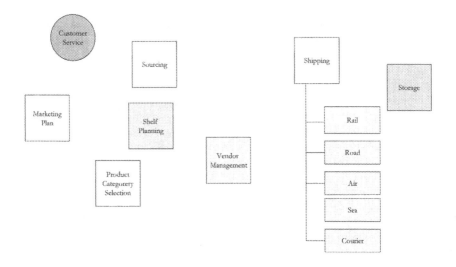

In a VBridged company:

- ✓ Vendor relationship will be balanced
- ✓ Environmental impacts on sustainability will be considered
- ✓ Value Profitability will drive decisions
- ✓ Inventory will decrease as the systems for buying are integrated with the company system for marketing
- ✓ Warehouse space will stabilize on a unit-cost basis as the inventory stabilizes as throughput increases

✓ Inventory and warehouse space will increase in balance with the consumer demand

✓ Transportation costs will be balanced due to business needs

✓ Balanced transportation costs will allow for investment in the business

✓ Purchase orders will be linked with the vendor systems so that raw material is ordered as required

Table 25

VBridged functions

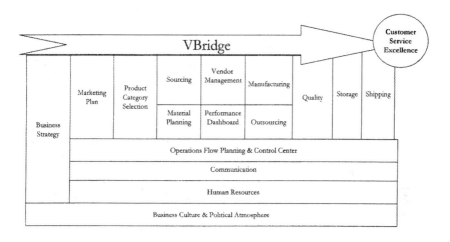

A VBridge organization requires managers with a high EOQ and an ability to deal with complexity. These managers must be dedicated to training and be able to communicate complex concepts. As Dick Parsons, former chairman and CEO of Time Warner, once said,

> "You want to surround yourself with the best people you can because being around smart people makes you better. When you have non-critical thinkers within the group, they are always chasing rabbits. They hinder the quality and the results of the discussion, because they ask the

wrong questions or focus on the wrong issues. This can ultimately limit what you as a group can achieve."[117]

Companies need managers grounded in honesty, ethical behavior, and political intensity focused on company development—managers who are equipped with analytical tools, knowledge, and intelligence about the environment, business, and the competition. This type of manager and management training is important as a VBridge is about taking processes from being relevant for the moment and striving to give them a longer-term relevance and designing and implementing a company message that consistently results in excellence, regardless of the audience's culture.

A VBridge moves us to a cultural integration that makes building bridges for communication, change, and driving for customer and business excellence the goal. VBridges are biomechanical, symbiotic organisms comprised of ten planks, six value components:

- ✓ People
- ✓ Processes
- ✓ Systems
- ✓ Operations
- ✓ Cost, Expense and Asset Management
- ✓ Profitability

and the V4L Learning Principles,[118] which we have made revisions to and incorporated into the model and which include:

- ✓ Variety—Product variety must be balanced with market demands and operational efficiency. Variety, or product differentiation, defines the flexibility you need in the Value Chain for marketing and buyer needs versus operational and Supply Chain effectiveness, where the more variety that exists the greater variability that will occur in the system.

✓ Velocity of Value Chain flows is the next key concept and manifests itself in all processes across the Value Chain. Velocity in the VBridge model affects the complete organization from, marketing to customer service to production to sales to supply chain and logistics. Velocity relates to our ability as an organization to achieve timely change from defining and implementing marketing plans to buying trips and converting merchant or customer needs to detailed designs, production plans and on-time in full delivery.

✓ Variability across the Value Chain is created by a lack of communication and control. Reducing variability allows the Supply Chain to operate with lower levels of inventory and fewer issues, and it allows your business to operate with less issues and noise as marketing, finance, and business needs are balanced with operational and Supply Chain constraints.

✓ VBridge visibility, incorporates Toyota's definition of visibility that is it is the use of correct metrics and the requirement for consensus across the team before plans are changed or implemented. Visibility in the Toyota model includes:

Performance Metrics have a 50 percent weigh for results and a 50 percent weight for process compliance. In other words, the goal is not to reward only short-term successes but to ensure that the correct processes are followed. Such an approach ensures that bottlenecks are visible and response immediate, changes deliberate, velocity is maintained.[119]

Table 26
VBridge Planks

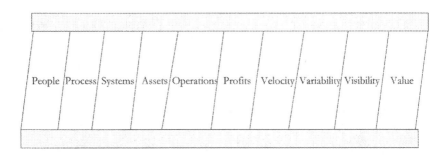

People	Process	Systems	Assets	Operations	Profits	Velocity	Variability	Visibility	Value

A VBridge organization is highly coordinated, as the concepts are not siloed but cross disciplinary. An integrated value chain or VBridge moves processes from being relevant for the moment and contextualizes them, giving a longer-term relevance and designing and implementing a company message that consistently results in excellence regardless of the audience's culture. Table 28 is a VBridge function map showing the functions that must be linked in VBridge and a simple transition flow showing how the VBridge model is built, starting from the Business Health Assessment and moving through different levels from individual areas to cross-functional communication to embedded expertise.

Table 27

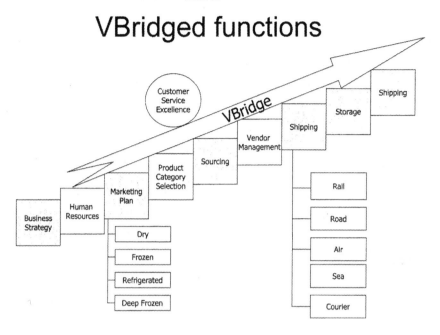

VBridged functions

A VBridge covers the spectrum of the business fluctuation from sales and marketing to shipping and exceeding customer needs. Most companies without an Integrated Value Chain Management (VBridge) strategic approach decouple their Value Chains into Logistics (warehousing and transportation) and Supply Chain (purchasing, inventory management, materials management, quality, and replenishment). When this occurs, companies lose the ability to function coherently. The VBridge is built around the integration of operational processes. This is a key reason for the cross-functional training.

The cross-functional training program called the "Milestones for Excellence" is a ten-step process in which business teams are trained to understand what they each do and the importance of coordination, collaboration, and communication along with learning the tenets of VBridge. This type of training approach showed me its value when implementing statistical process control, which required designing and training staff in statistical methods to improve quality. Key elements of the Milestone for Excellence program training relate to creating:

✓ Training in business, supply chain, and logistics and the synergies that are required for effective operations
✓ Standardized work
✓ Standard Operating Procedures
✓ Business operation control center development and creation

Table 28

VBridge Implementation Steps

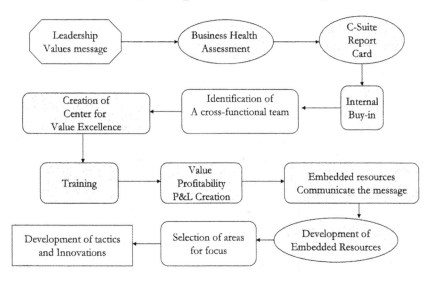

Strategy

A VBridge organization is an integrated, interconnected organization that is cost, consumer, and environmentally centered. There are trade-offs, but the way to balance the trade-offs is to understand the two consumers every organization services—existing consumers and next-generation consumers.

Table 29

VBridge Strategic Focus

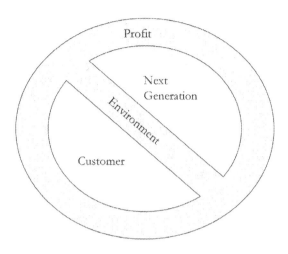

Existing consumers are the ones you presently service. Next-generation consumers are the ones impacted by the sustainability decisions you make today and to whom you will be selling tomorrow. Taking this approach changes your perspective as well as your strategic marketing plans as you view the needs of today's consumers and products through the lens of the impact on future consumers who, while needing a different product mix, will be seeing and reaping the results of today's products. These next-generation customers will make a decision on buying your products based on the reputation you have in the future and based on the impact on the environment and their lives that your past products have had. This is why business strategy, product development, and marketing strategy are key parts of the VBridge and integral to building the communication process bridge.

You should do a forward-looking strategy process flow and a backward flow through your organization and leadership to ensure the validity of the VBridge you are building. As each business selects different alternatives, strategies have to be covered within the context of the organization and Value Profitability. However, the planning, regardless of the strategic alternative, needs to address one, two, five, and ten-year plans. An example of a backward strategic review would be how your existing strategy and processes have functioned in the last 6 months to a year, which you can get from the Business Health Assessment. Reviewing a major sales program will also enable you to identify strategic and tactical issues and areas where your communication and management processes are working well. To ensure this occurs, VBridge organizations utilize the Centers of Value Excellence reviewed before, which include C-suite staff at monthly meetings. In addition, VBridge updates are provided at each business board meeting. In the end, the VBridge must be integrated and part of the company strategy.

Supply Chain

One lesson that people usually carry away from the classical beer game is that structure drives behavior. In a VBridge Supply Chain, all the tools of the Supply Chain from Quality, Lean, and Theory of Constraints to Six Sigma can be utilized. However, those are only tools, not the structure. The VBridge structure is layered for strength, building on prior elements and cross-supported as the elements of process are taught, embedded, and internalized. A marketing department that is part of a VBridge-driven organization can discuss the Supply Chain and marketing needs with similar strength—what changes is the degree of focus. The best analogy in science is where you have biochemists and geophysicists. In the same way, once a VBridge takes hold of an organization, Marklogisticians will start to integrate marketing and logistics so that the marketing department will have people on board who can aid and focus them on marketing while also having a sub-specialization in logistics. Of equal importance, the VBridge integrates marketing and product decisions into the supply-chain design to make it more efficient and effective. Product design and packaging parameters are critical to reducing waste while maximizing shelf space for a smaller retail pack size, providing reduced product costs for the manufacturer and reduced capital costs for the retailer.

The integration of the VBridge philosophy into a standard business changes its focus, making the entire organization more effective and efficient as it focuses on reducing overall costs and resource utilization across the entire Value Chain. Smaller products that utilize less resources but which provide the same or improved benefits will fit in with a smaller transportation and warehousing footprint. Transitioning from standard forecasting to new processes allows for the development of a new organizational perspective, resulting in the delivery of greater value for the organization with reduced resource utilization. Initially, this process will provide organizations adapting the VBridge process a cost advantage as they translate this into value for workers and consumers.

A VBridge focus reduces waste, not just in the supply chain with reduced lead times, less asset use, and increased development of people. It increases velocity, variability, visibility, and value. Let's look at a few key areas.

System Integration

Enterprise Resource Planning (ERP) systems such as SAP, Manugistics, Peoplesoft, Oracle, and JD Edwards are increasingly been linked into specialized warehouse management systems (WMS) such as Red Prairie and Delfour. In addition, transportation management systems, along with the WMS, have been linked into the ERP systems of companies. Systems represent a significant investment for any company and at the end still will not address the customer's needs if the training and system expertise are not in place. As a rule, it is better to have a system that people understand, know how to use, and can provide a high case fill with than the latest and greatest software version that they do not understand and which was only implemented at the high cost of a operational issue and staff who you had to terminate and later have to rehire. The system needs to function with the business and teamwork flow so organizational functions are integrated.

Demand Forecasting

The most important aspect of any part of supply chain and logistics is the forecast for dependent and independent demand. All other aspects of the Value Chain from finance, profit, revenue, and supply chain to logistics are dependent on the forecast. If the forecast is wrong, you will build the incorrect size warehouses and make or buy the wrong product. Many forecasts have very low accuracies, in the range of 50 to 65 percent. However, forecasts as high as 85 to 90 percent can be achieved if properly trained people, organization processes, and systems are in place. The cost of forecast error includes:

- ✓ Capital
- ✓ Marketing
- ✓ Operational overhead
- ✓ Warehousing
- ✓ Transportation
- ✓ Customer service
- ✓ Wasted products
- ✓ Write-offs
- ✓ Disposal costs

Minimizing poor forecasts should be a focus at every company. Forecasts affect what we make, build, buy, store, move, and dispose of. One of the fastest ways to reduce costs is to increase forecast accuracy. Forecasting starts with marketing and sales in manufacturing environments and with marketing, store operations, merchants, and replenishment in retailing. In both cases, access to point of sale information benefits and allows the organization to make better and wiser decisions. The ultimate in forecast improvement, however, is to eliminate forecasts by turning instead to one of the three types of demand listed below.

✓ Build to demand is used by manufacturers building specific equipment. However, it can be utilized and refined to a much greater degree with the tools we have today. Look at www.Deere.com, where you can select and adjust online the components for your equipment.

✓ Ship to demand is what we do with Ecom businesses, where the product is shipped based on confirmed orders.

✓ Pick up on demand.

As we said earlier, we have the capability to do all three processes, especially the last two given Web tools available today. The standard process is shown below:

Table 30

Simplified Classical Manufacturing Forecasting

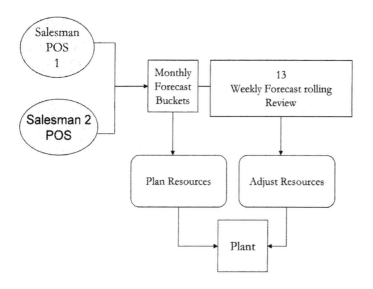

Key to forecasting is the ability and flexibility to adjust the forecasts' rate of response to changes.[120] This can be done by developing for Brick and Mortar stores the use of lower Tiered multi-nodal neural network Supply Chain and Logistics applications.

Sales Team Integration

Demand and Supply systems need to be integrated. This goes beyond just having demand analysts and supply analysts or managers and directors. Sales personnel must become an extension of the operational side of the business. Sales personnel need to be measured not only on the success of the account in terms of sales but on their accounts' fill rate and order line-on time in full rate. Bonuses for personnel need to have crossfunctional business measures that motivate sales personnel to become experts in supply systems so that they understand all aspects of what is required to ensure that the right product in the right amount is made and delivered at the right time. It is not enough just to say, "I need a product on a specific date," tell the salesperson, and then leave it. Retailers need to ensure that companies have support teams for their accounts, where everyone on the team is copied on what has been agreed to so that nothing is dropped. While the salesperson will coordinate his or her support team, in the end the team needs to be reporting to the customer. The customer, both at the start and the finish of any process, needs to have input and feedback to ensure that processes are continuing to drive forward.

Sourcing, Cost, and Price

Cost and price relationships are key components of the VBridge and need to be valued with Natural Capital without being a brake on profitability. Item proliferation also plays a role in this, as increasing the number of items and changing product design constantly has an impact on the resource cost of items. Companies that have many nonconsumable short product life items, for example, sellers of cell phones, will increasingly face issues with input and disposal costs. This applies to cell phones, and computers which have relative high values and margins, and the peripheral equipment, which are increasingly lower priced. Increasing item proliferation and decreasing product life increases business and social costs and reduces our ability to address variability, while increasing the amount of shipping that takes place.

To address item proliferation in short shelf life products, companies providing such items require a forum to discuss options and ways to move out of a market without many of them doing so at the same time. Some options these manufacturers have include intelligently segmenting their product lines into products that can be moved up scale via Product development and Product life cycle management designing for a longer life cycle by adjusting the design parameters and quality. This change could then be transferred to their brand marketing so they achieve higher opening value recognition and price points with quality and ergonomic design. The message here to those buying at the low price point is we provide higher level products that will reduce your overall costs. Basically "Better products, save money and create a healthier environment". In line with this change, we have already started to see some companies develop products such as this on a small scale for the higher end market.

There will however always be a place for low-end price point products with shorter life spans and this is where designing for recycling will be important. Smaller items that can be reused can still be designed for this market. However the difference in value will soon become clear once the actual environmental impact is factored in.

To address demand spikes and the spreading flux resulting from item proliferation, purchasing decision planning processes such as Collaborative Forecasting and Planning (CPFR) joined with manufacturing processes to handle inaccurate forecasts, short production runs, and product customization will be the difference between the successful companies and the ones that fail. Collaborative Forecasting and Planning was initially a Nine Step process stemming from a project Walmart, SAP, Manugistics and consulting firm Benchmarking Partners initiated. The program has now been transformed into a four step process. However while the process is needed the adaptation of it and its success has been a struggle due to its apparent complexity. Still companies need to adapt processes such as CPFR while ensuring that when implementing they have a detailed planning process and project team who understand the process. There are also fairly standard processes incorporated into ERP sytems, that work well if trained and knowledgeable staff and managers are utilized. However often training is a major impediment. This jumped out to me at a meeting with a company's key vice president and directors, unfortunately none knew the answers to some very simple material management questions. Knowledge and training are one of the largest obstacles we face to transforming companies for profit especially at the upper to mid-management levels. However without training at the highest levels it will be difficult for managers to know how to hirer properly trained and qualified staff. As resources and transportation becomes more difficult, it will be even more important to have the right product where you want it when you need it. The training and knowledge of your staff will increasing be the dividing line between successful companies who innovate and transform and those who lag behind. The issue is that with the challenges we face we need to work together and those who have the staff and the ability need to work with those who don't to aide them. Colleges and Universities can also assist in this however in many cases they do not have the ability to discern good processes from bad as many have never worked in industry.

Customers of both retail and wholesale will face increasing issues keeping their shelves full if they do not invest the money and time in development and sustainability. Corporations need to ensure that the information is driven both up and across the organization on methods, processes, and means of ensuring that systems and supply personnel know what to do. In many cases, personnel have been trained in APIC courses and yet do not have the ability to implement in the real world the applications that are needed. Creation of Centers of Value Excellence facilitates the training of specialists who can drive improvement in this area via systems using the VBridge and the Milestone for Excellence program.

Cost and price delivered via sourcing will always be a key variable, as it:

- ✓ Is externally focused
- ✓ Aims to maximize total value
- ✓ Requires internal cross-functional co-ordination

VBridge integrated functions include:

- ✓ Sales information (promotions planning, new products, product development)
- ✓ Forecasting
- ✓ Production scheduling
- ✓ Finished inventory planning
- ✓ Purchasing
- ✓ Distribution center planning
- ✓ Customer inventory allocation (dynamic vs. static allocation)
- ✓ Transportation planning
- ✓ Carrier Website PO tracking
- ✓ Customer notification
- ✓ Quality information

To put this information into perspective, we need to remember that as business people we sell dreams, not just products, to people. It is people who buy our products and innovations. I remember one class where a professor taught that the user of a drill buys not the drill but the dream of the holes that the drill will make. We risk all as businesspeople if we forget the lesson that consumers buy dreams and forget the resource and employment reality underlying their purchases. The employment reality being consumers are workers requiring employment. While retailers and big box stores can utilize the psychological knowledge that companies have gained over the years to translate a visit into a buying decision, it is people we bring into our stores to look at our products. If the products and processes of stores are shown to have an increasingly detrimental impact on the American and European consumer/workers' ability to survive, the environment, and our long-term standard of living, people will make new decisions on where and what to spend their dollars on.

Value Profitability, Business Health Assessments, VBridge Integrated Value Chain Management, and Milestones for Excellence programs are all processes and tools to achieve change, focusing business and governments on transformation to achieve sustainable profitable businesses while addressing the trends affecting our planet. Over the years, I have seen and negotiated multi-million dollar contracts, and each decision has been based on dollars and cents. Profit is the name of the game. We are in business to make money. However, businesspeople are not crazy. If you have a business and the business is in an area where there are forest fires, you had better believe the businesspeople will stop selling product to go and fight the fire. The reality is that in business you need both a long-term and short-term outlook. The short-term one says, "If I keep selling while the houses in front of me burn, I will make some money." The long-term perspective says, "If I don't put out the house fires in front of me, I may make a few bucks more, though my house and my business will burn down and then I will sell nothing." Let's put out the fire with the support of a new business model.

Chapter 9:
Detailed Broad Trends and Resources

This chapter contains more material on the top five broad trends summarized in chapter 4. Prior to writing this, I researched the alternative views on these subjects, and none contradicts the basic facts we discuss from population increases, peak oil, climate change, and food crisis to environmental issues and cancer. The more research I did, the more it was obvious that we face potentially tragic consequences if the population does not recognize the issues and address them.

Unfortunately, pure selfish motivation will often get people moving when care and concern for others does not succeed. The world is counterintuitive. Today we are in the situation where a lot of people have taken a short-term outlook, as they do not have the information to know that the houses around them are burning fast. The purpose of this book is to help people understand that not only are the houses around them burning, but also the building we are in has caught fire! We need to fight the fire now, not tomorrow—now! If we do not buy a fire engine and start pumping water, we will lose our business and more. In the *Art of War*, Sun Tzu wrote over 2,400 years ago, "What enables the wise ruler and the good general (leader) to strike and conquer and achieve things beyond the reach of ordinary men is foreknowledge." What Sun Tzu wrote then is still true today!

Foreknowledge can be acquired by blog research reviewing, discourse analysis, semiotic analysis, ethnographic analysis, and need-style analysis. You have word-of-mouth research using staff or loyalty programs. You can then segment all of this data in a variety of ways. What you do with the data is critical.

Trend 1: Climate Change

In 2003, my wife and I were flying into Hong Kong through dark, threatening storm clouds. Only when we landed were we able to look up and see that what we had taken for storm clouds was in fact smog that had drifted over and around Hong Kong from Shenzhen. While there are questions about what carbon is doing to the environment, you only need to see it to understand what a large carbon footprint we have created by forcing global manufacturing into southern China and that this is a microcosm of what we may face if our behavior continues. Global climate change has been in the news over the last few years, initially popularized by Al Gore as global warming in his book, *An Inconvenient Truth*,[121] in which he depicted massive changes in the climate that would affect populations. One key passage that jumped out at me from the book was the words:

> "The relationship between human civilization and the Earth has been utterly transformed by a combination of factors, including the population explosion, the technical revolution and a willingness to ignore the future consequences of our present actions. The underlying reality is that we are colliding with the planet's ecological systems and its most vulnerable components are crumbling as a result."[122]

Humanity is colliding with the planet. Instead of a cooperative, stewardship approach of resources, we have clear-cut the planet. As the human population increases, our use of the biosphere has grown significantly. Where we once utilized limited ecological areas such as plains and forests, leaving many available for animals, most are now utilized to create food for city populations. We are restructuring animals daily into smaller, less viable niches. This is a significant part of the reason for the concern regarding what changing weather will do to populations. For example, Bangladesh in the fifteenth century had a smaller population compared to today. Their population has increased to the point that it is the seventh most populated country in the world where large numbers of people are impacted by storms. In the chart below, you can see Bangladesh's projected population to 2050.

Bangladesh   Table 31
Population (thousands)
Medium variant
1950–2050

Year	Population
1950	43 595
1955	48 442
1960	54 138
1965	60 931
1970	69 178
1975	79 049
1980	90 397
1985	102 993
1990	115 632
1995	128 086
2000	140 767
2005	153 122
2010	164 425
2015	175 217
2020	185 552
2025	195 012
2030	203 214
2035	209 929
2040	215 339
2045	219 589
2050	222 495

Source: Population Division of the Department of Economic and Social Affairs of the United Nations Secretariat, *World Population Prospects: The 2008 Revision*, http://esa.un.org/unpp, Sunday, February 07, 2010; 8:37:32 AM.

As the global population increases, Climate change will have an increasing impact on humanity. *Civilization and Climate*[123] was a great title for E. Huntington's book on the impact of climate on weather. Today, we could refer to the present situation as a clash of consuming civilizations as Westerners have taken our consumption patterns to an extreme, and Asians are coming up behind us. At one time, the climate was seen as controlled by God. Now we have appropriated for ourselves the ability to influence the climate and the earth. We have taken command of a situation with little or no knowledge of what we are doing. Many see business and Western civilization as destroyers of the earth and frame climate change as catastrophic and destructive.

Western science at one time was seen as a means to know and understand God and the universe. Today, we tend to see science as a means to destroy the earth. Business and government are the gatekeepers for how this scientific knowledge will be used for good or evil. This is why some favor the description that we live in an anthropogenic era, where we face four alternatives:

- ✓ Do nothing, continuing our present ways of operating and hope the global outcome is favorable.
- ✓ Try to stabilize our growth at present levels and hope the outcome is favorable.
- ✓ Try to stabilize or control the situation so we can control the impact as we grow.
- ✓ Work to set the climate and environment back to a level more conducive for people.

Each alternative represents a cultural and economic decision that will affect your business. We have seen and will see over time a change in the climate. The question is what to do about it. There is very little open scientific debate on what is causing climate change (see Climate-gate). What we will do here is give you a brief overview. However, regardless of the position scientists take, they all agree that the world's climate is changing. A silent minority, however, does not agree on the cause. This is important for two reasons:

Regardless of the cause, you face a major problem to your business.

The solution posed by the majority of scientists will pose a challenge for your business that you will need to start addressing now.

In 1979, the US National Academy of Scientists' Climate Research Board convened an ad hoc study group on carbon dioxide and climate. The report, which became known as the Charney Report, is very interesting reading, as such a small group created a very well-written report. They assessed a doubling of carbon as having a 3-degree impact plus or minus 1.5 degrees Celsius. Today one of the most publicized and documented sources on climate change, although one facing increasing debate between proponents of a climate change extreme case and those supporting a lesser climate change scenario, is the United Nations Intergovernmental Panel on Climate Change (IPCC). To understand the IPCC reporting, you need to understand that climate change and its challenges are based on climate change theories and modeling. While no one can say that an individual weather event is caused by climate change, many thousands of scientists around the world worked together in 1990 to create in 1990 the first IPCC assessment report. This report was not the first of its kind on global warming, but it was the first globally recognized, UN-authorized report. The report identified that civilization (in the majority Western civilization, you and I) had generated sufficient greenhouse gas particles to affect atmospheric conditions in a significant way.

The IPCC review process normally takes place in three stages for the procedures for the preparation for the report:

1) Expert review of IPCC reports,
2) Government/expert review of IPCC reports, and
3) Government review of the summaries for policymakers, overview chapters and/or the synthesis report.

The third item is the most critical, as most people only review the summary, not the technical report.

In 1992, the United Nations Framework Convention on Climate Change was created to stabilize the greenhouse gas concentrations at a level that would prevent human interference in the climate systems. The goal was to ensure that ecosystems could adapt naturally to changes and to prevent food-production issues. There have been a variety of major conferences on the subject to generate awareness, such as the:

1992 Rio Earth Summit held in Rio de Janeiro

1996 Second IPCC Assessment Report

1997 adoption of the Kyoto Protocol

2001 Third IPCC Assessment Report

2005 Hurricane Katrina

2006 *An Inconvenient Truth* is released to theaters

2007 Release of the fourth IPCC Assessment Report

One thing the fourth IPCC report did was to make it clear where the report writers stood on the subject of global warnings. They stated,

"Warming of the climate system is unequivocal, as is now evident from observations of increases in global average air and ocean temperatures, widespread melting of snow and ice and rising global average sea level."[124]

As we continue to review global warming, it is critical to note that even scientists not in agreement with the causes of global warming, such as Roy W. Spenser,[125] are in agreement that "there is very little scientific disagreement over the fact that the extra carbon dioxide mankind is emitting is causing a slight enhancement of the Earth's natural greenhouse gas effect. What is disputed is how the atmosphere will respond in terms of feedback."[126] Key to these discussions and planning are the IPCC reports, whose mandate is to "assess on a comprehensive, objective and transparent basis the scientific, technical and socio-economic information relevant to understanding the scientific basis of risk of human induced climate change."[127]

Analysis and study of the impact of humankind on the atmospheric composition and later weather has taken place over some time. Svante August Arrhenius (1859-1927), a Noble Prize winner, formulated the mathematical theories of the impact of carbon on temperatures, as shown below.

$$\Delta F = \alpha \ln(C/C_0)$$

His theory did not factor in other changes, and he theorized that the warming would be good for the earth. However, scientists differ on that point. In 1906, Arrhenius theorized that the earth would warm with a doubling of carbon by 1.6 degrees in about three thousand years. However, the human increase in carbon use has advanced the doubling rate to once every one hundred years. John Tyndale (1820-1893) and Guy Callender (1898-1964) also contributed to theories of global warming with their work. Callender also saw global warming as a positive for the earth. This, however, has changed with the IPCC reports, which see carbon increases as detrimental.

Below is a table showing the composition of the earth's atmospere.[128]

TABLE 32
Average composition of the atmosphere up to an altitude of 25 km.

Gas Name	Chemical Formula	Percent Volume
Nitrogen	N2	78.08%
Oxygen	O2	20.95%
*Water	H2O	0 to 4%
Argon	Ar	0.93%
*Carbon Dioxide	CO2	0.0360%
Neon	Ne	0.0018%
Helium	He	0.0005%
*Methane	CH4	0.00017%
Hydrogen	H2	0.00005%
*Nitrous Oxide	N2O	0.00003%
*Ozone	O3	0.000004%

* variable gases

You can see the different types of gases that make up the atmosphere. Nitrogen and oxygen are the key particles in the atmosphere. It is important, therefore, to understand that there are many other factors aside from carbon that can affect the global climate, some of which are listed below:

Energy from the sun, which is located at the center of our solar system, warms the earth and provides the energy needed for photosynthesis. The energy picked up by the earth varies during the year. Outgoing infrared radiation cools the earth as the earth reflects radiation back into space. Absorbed sunlight must be balanced by reflected infrared radiation for the earth to remain cool. Everything on earth is continually absorbing and emitting energy. To model this, a radioactive transfer model has to be used because the interplay of factors is so complex. This changing emission of radiation also supports the movement of air currents.

Cloud cover also has an impact on the amount of radiation absorbed and emitted by the earth. In one case, it shields the earth, and in the other, it blocks the radiation of absorbed heat.

Oceans are critical to climate change as they absorb carbon and can increase water vapor in the atmosphere.

Water vapor is an important factor in how the earth's temperatures increases, and many climate models hold water vapor constant, where Minschwaner & Dessler's model predicts increasing temperatures to increase humidity, but not to the degree assumed by many climate models.[129] Oxygen, Methane, and Nitrous Oxide produced in the main from fertilizers and other greenhouse gases act as a screen, changing the atmospheric temperatures between the lower and upper atmosphere. Ozone, land use, and halocarbons all have an affect. Aerosols, which are very small particles in the air, also influence the result. Fires, sand storms, volcanoes, and the burning of fossil fuels can create aerosols. Aerosols usually cool the global area below them, with the largest example of this being the severe volcanic eruption of Mount Pinatubo in the Philippines in 1991, where large amounts of aerosol were emitted into the stratosphere, possibly causing summer temperatures to be cooler than normal. "Scientists estimate that Mount Pinatubo injected about 20 million tons of sulfur dioxide into the atmosphere, cooling average global temperatures over the following year by about half a degree."[130]

The Icelandic volcano eruption in April 2010 is another example of this. Three greenhouse gases not shown above but which are managed under the Kyoto Protocol are: Hydro fluorocarbons, Perfluorocarbons, and Sulphur hexafluoride.

All of these factors must be addressed by any climate model if the model is to be accurate. Scientists on the Intergovernmental Panel on Climate Change (IPCC) believe we have an excellent understanding of the climate forcing caused by humans. However, accuracy, as we know, is very hard to come by, as computer modeling is what is used and the models are only as accurate as the information and history we have been able to record to create a statistical record. The IPCC and other reports are all based on statistics gathered over the last one hundred years, during which we were also changing the location and process of measuring temperature. This means that what we have is a directional guide to change. At the same time, the human forcing of the climate is impacted by other things we have done, such as the ozone depletion, which at one time was a serious problem. Ozone depletion in 1985 was identified as a critical issue in creating ozone holes, and in 1987, a UN resolution was passed to control it.

Carbon, which we are measuring, accounts for 380 parts per million at present, or 380 molecules of carbon make up every million particles of air. While large amounts of carbon are moved around in the atmosphere between the air and the ocean, which act as heat sinks, the evidence suggests that human activity, which is what the IPCC reports are reviewing, is having an impact. What that impact is and the accuracy of the models is what has caused "Climate-gate," an article in the *Times Online*, January 17, 2010, which called into question portions of the IPCC report.

The theory that climate change will melt most of the Himalayan glaciers by 2035 is likely to be retracted. A central claim supporting this theory was based on a news story in the *New Scientist*, a popular science journal, published before the IPCC's 2007 report. The *New Scientist* report was based on a short telephone interview with Syed Hasnain, a scientist based at Jawaharlal Nehru University in Delhi. Syed retracted the report based on the work of a Canadian geologist Graham Cogley. The point is there are concerns with climate modeling, however, even those who debate it still agree that there has been a change in the global temperatures to a higher level. What that means is the issue. Below is an extract from Table SPM 2 of regional proposed changes from the 2007 IPCC synthesis report.

Asia   By the 2050s, freshwater availability in Central, South, and
             Southeast Asia, particularly in large river basins, is projected
             to decrease. Coastal areas, especially heavily populated
             megadelta regions in South, East, and Southeast Asia, will be
             at greatest risk due to increased flooding from the sea and,
             in some megadeltas, flooding from the rivers.

Europe   Climate change is expected to magnify regional differences
             in Europe's natural resources and assets. Negative impacts
             will include increased risk of inland flash floods and more
             frequent coastal flooding and increased erosion (due to
             storminess and sea level rise).
             In southern Europe, climate change is projected to worsen
             conditions (high temperatures and drought) in a region
             already vulnerable to climate variability, and to reduce water
             availability, hydropower potential, summer tourism, and, in
             general, crop productivity.

Latin   By mid-century, increases in temperature and associated
America decreases in soil water are projected to lead to gradual
             replacement of tropical forest by savanna in eastern
             Amazonia. Semi-arid vegetation will tend to be replaced by
             arid-land vegetation. There is a risk of significant
             biodiversity loss through species extinction in many areas of
             tropical Latin America.

North   Warming in western mountains is projected to cause
America decreased snowpack, more winter flooding, and reduced
             summer flows, exacerbating competition for over-allocated
             water resources. In the early decades of the century,
             moderate climate change is projected to increase aggregate
             yields of rain-fed agriculture by 5 to 20%, but with
             important variability among regions. Major challenges are
             projected for crops that are near the warm end of their
             suitable range or which depend on highly utilized water
             resources.

Polar   The main projected biophysical effects are reductions in
Regions thickness and extent of glaciers, ice sheets, and sea ice, and
             changes in natural ecosystems with detrimental effects on
             many organisms including migratory birds, mammals, and
             higher predators.   Table 33

Note: Unless stated explicitly, all entries are from Working Group II SPM text and are either very high confidence or high confidence statements, reflecting different sectors (agriculture, ecosystems, water, coasts, health, industry, and settlements).

Based on the report, you can see major changes proposed for different areas. The industrial revolution started about 150 years ago. During the intervening time, as we increased the use of energy we have increased our carbon use. Presently, a net 6.2 billion metric tons (7.2 billion metric tons less 1 billion metric tons of sinks) of anthropogenic carbon dioxide emissions are produced each year (measured in carbon-equivalent terms), and an estimated 4.1 billion metric tons are added to the atmosphere each year.[131] To address the increasing parts per million of carbon in the atmosphere will require major changes in the way we generate and use energy. The Value Chain is the key area that will require and face the most changes.

Trend 2: The End of Environmentally Low-Impact Easy Oil

Petroleum resources started becoming more critical in the nineteenth century with the birth of the plastic industry in 1839, when Charles Goodyear discovered an early version of plastic. Twelve years later, his brother Nelson invented "Ebonite."[132] This preceded the first US rock oil rush in the 1850s, which George Bissell started with the idea of drilling for rock oil and using it as an illuminator.[133] This in turn led to the development of Standard Oil, Shell Oil, and other companies that drilled for and sold oil. Oil became an increasingly global resource with Ludwig Nobel's idea of bulk shipping in large tanks, an idea improved upon by Marcus Samuel, the father of Shell Oil. While the invention of electric illumination hurt the oil markets, the invention of the combustion engine in the early nineteenth century drove demand for oil and its derivatives to fuel automobiles, trains, and planes, giving the petroleum industry a roaring boost that has not stopped. Oil began to be used for civilian requirements and took on strategic importance in World War I and II.[134] World energy consumption tripled between 1949 and 1972, and oil consumption increased by five times.[135] Oil usage worldwide has increased dramatically at the same time that oil reserves in the United States have been almost exhausted and the world has shifted from coal to oil. The total amount of oil extracted from the world's underground, limited oil reserves have grown since 1859 from a "few thousand barrels a year to 65 million barrels per day by the end of the twentieth century."[136] To meet this demand, the discovery of oil in Arabia in 1931 was critical. Charles R. Crane and Karl S. Twitchell were commissioned to carry out the first American geological survey, and they reported a strong probability of oil deposits.[137] This discovery would significantly impact world politics. Standard Oil[138] and the Rockefellers, with the cooperation of Al Saud and the help of St. John Philby, created a contract for Saudi Arabian oil. The actual discovery of oil in 1938 and Roosevelt's meeting with Ibn Saud in 1945 cemented United States involvement in the area. The United States would agree to fully back and support a country and a religious group, Wahhabism, within Islam that it did not understand. This support has continued almost unabated during the creation of OPEC (1960) and the first use of oil as a weapon in the 1967 Six-Day War. The need for oil to supply all of the West's and most of the East's need for fuel has left the world at the mercy of oil and natural gas and the countries that provide it.

Schumacher was the first to identify and argue against the dependence on oil. "The richest and cheapest reserves are located in some of the world's most unstable countries," he wrote. "Faced with such uncertainty, it is tempting o abandon the quest for a long-term view and simply to hope for the best."[139] The oil industry has worked diligently to satisfy and also develop the demand for oil, which is driven by the newest and latest inventions, which require electricity, and by a prosperity in which people always want more, requiring transportation and supply chains to depend increasingly on transportation that uses oil. In the 1970s, the United States went from restricting oil imports to actively removing quotas and increasing imports. The two oil shocks of the seventies, the Yom Kippur OPEC oil embargo of 1973 and then with the war in Iran, resulted in short-term attempts to change this dependency, though nothing significantly changed. The first split with Japan and the United States on foreign policy came about due to oil and support for Israel.[140] Since then, oil prices have fluctuated, and we have had not one but two Gulf wars. However, while in the first two cases Western countries pursued strategies to effectively put in place conservation and change to alternative sources, this has not continued. At the same time, governments and oil and automobile companies, instead of promoting the "small is beautiful" idea of Schumacher, increasingly rolled out SUVs that consumed this non-renewable resource as if it was water. This is not only the responsibility of the corporations but of people who neglect the lessons of the past.

The instability of the Middle East has only increased, due not only to oil special interest groups and government shortsightedness, but also due to Middle Easterners' desire to control their own future in their own way. Yet, in the midst of all this history, governments continue to deny the obvious—that we are in the Middle East to support our civilization's energy needs. James Placke, an American diplomat and economic officer at the US Embassy in Baghdad and petroleum officer in the US embassy in Tripoli in 1970, made the point that, "Control of the flow of resources has been of strategic concern through history. Asserting control over a vital source of energy would permit Middle Eastern states to regain the power position vis-à-vis the West, which this area lost long ago."[141] We have forgotten what Placke, Schumacher, and so many others tried to teach us. Oil is still king in the global market, and increasingly the demand and need for oil will lead to instability as the West and increasingly the rest of the world has to deal with the question of energy or security.[142]

Corporations have the opportunity now to promote corporate conservationism and new technologies to replace oil. Corporations which fail to do so will be placing themselves in the path of economic devastation as oil resources are quickly exhausted as demand is accelerated by the increase in Chinese prosperity. Governments and corporations in the West, therefore, have two significant reasons to promote conservation and new technologies.

Reason 1

The majority of terrorism that Western countries and the United States face is from Middle Eastern countries that resent the presence of Western armies on their soil. However, the real resentment is not from the poor in the Middle East, but from religious, mostly middle-class Islamists who resent, fear, and hate having Western and especially US armies on their soil. By developing different sources of energy, we could significantly reduce not only our carbon footprint but also the money funding terrorism by reducing the demand and price of oil based on a simple demand and supply theory. This would reduce our need for a military presence in the Middle East and thus the dangers we face from a terrorist attack. It would also mean that countries that protest so vehemently against US and Western needs could be motivated to do business as the lifestyles of the population are funded by the West's and increasingly Asian need for oil.

Reason 2

Opinions differ on when oil will peak and decline, as oil is not a renewable resource. The length of time estimated by M. King Hubbert, Colin J. Campbell, and Jean Laherrere vary; however, it may be between 2006 and 2015.[143] Campbell's most prominent and influential publication was the article "The End of Cheap Oil?" published in the March 1998 issue of *Scientific American*. The coauthor of that article, Jean Laherrere, had worked for the oil company Total (now Total Fina Elf) for thirty-seven years in a variety of roles, encompassing exploration activities in the Sahara, Australia, Canada, and Paris.[144]

While some such as Peter Huber and Bjorn Lomberg disagree with the decline in oil, the potential impact of this on global civilizations must be considered and planned for. With the majority of accessible oil reserves in the Middle East or close to China, the supply lines to Western civilization are dependent on the continuation of governments in the Middle East that favor the United States and the West. Should the low estimates of oil's life as a viable energy source be correct, with the dependence of all methods of travel on this source of energy, any significant decline could and probably will result in political instability in such countries and war. The United States' strategy of maintaining a military presence in the Middle East thus makes military sense. However, supply lines are limited and long, and any force projection into the region will require tremendous amounts of oil to maintain. Since ignoring the indigenous religious basis of Islam, angers Muslims' and tends to radicalize Muslim populations who control significant oil resources we need to review the way we relate to Muslim populations and governments. If Western governments and specifically the United States, Britain, and the Anglo-Saxon component of Western civilization ignore these considerations, not only will we lose the years when we can be dependent on good will. We may also lose the ability to bring those civilizations onto our side and reap instead a whirlwind of hate and anger at a time when we will not be able to afford it. We may also reap internal destabilization at home, given the millions of Muslims that are now present in Western countries and growing.

Given the above, it is amazing the small amount of detailed information we get from the media such as CNN and other news agencies on the impact of oil on politics, when in fact highly placed special interest groups have a focus on this area. Historically, there are three major reasons for Western interest in the Middle East:

- ✓ Jerusalem as the center of Christian and Jewish beginnings
- ✓ Oil
- ✓ Opposition to other political entities

Most Western countries downplay the role oil plays in influencing Western interest in Middle Eastern politics, an approach and statement that are

100 percent counterintuitive. Modern civilization is an energy-based one, and we get most of that energy from oil. The United States has 5 percent of the world's oil and consumes 25 percent of the world's production annually. There is a good reason to be in the Middle East, as we discussed above, however, there is an even better reason to promote conservation and alternate technologies while there is still time. One of the key things my department did in the world's largest company was track the cost and price of diesel and oil. Not because we bought oil to sell to consumers but because everything we moved, everything we touched and wanted to sell required a movement that required an expense in oil and diesel. All of those products you see in every store require the consumption of fuel to move it, whether by ship, rail, or road, and that consumption comes at a hefty price. If it goes too high, that price can dramatically shift profitability, even for the largest companies. Below is the energy use in the United States. As you can see, 28 percent of energy is used for Transportation.

Table 34   **Share of Enerrgy Used for Transportation, 2008**

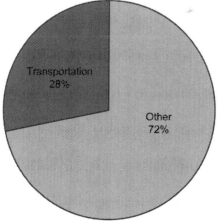

Source: Energy Information Administration
Annual Energy Review 2008.

Reiner Kummel identified how our consumption of energy has created an extraordinary amount of free work as energy basically creates energy servants for us. Think about going to the store. You can select to walk, ride a bicycle, or drive to the store. Walking and cycling require the conversion of food to energy for our bodies, but by driving we use less physical energy and use the energy conversion from gas to power our vehicles to go to the store. This use of mechanical energy servants such as cars not only requires the consumption of more energy, but it also results in our decreased physical health. Based on the joules (energy) we consume, one can identify how many energy servants we, as an economy, use.[145] While scientists have identified that energy conversion has improved,[146] our culture in the last 150 years of the Industrial Revolution has grown based on a Value Chain model of cheap fuel to achieve higher mechanization and faster speeds, lowering the costs of inputs and outputs as we move resources around the world to support our economy. Our value chain has been built on being able to move raw materials and resources to fixed manufacturing locations and distributing products from those locations to the cities, which have become our consumption nodes, and the countryside. We have built a networked society where the population involved in farming has dropped as the cities have increased as nodes of consumption. The resources to support this change from concrete highways to heating energy distribution has been built to support these changes. This model of consumption nodes, while supporting the increase in energy efficiency as distribution costs have been reduced, means that we are increasing the amount of food moved from the country to the city. It also means that as we have shifted jobs and production to China, our global economy has become heavily dependent on easily accessible, low environmental impact energy, which we define as energy extracted from global oil resources where the environment at extraction is not affected.

Energy is critical to the survival of the human race, with the majority of the energy used coming from three sources:

✓ Burning wood
✓ Burning coal
✓ Burning oil (biological)

Initially, our energy use was solely for non-technological uses:

✓ Cooking
✓ Heating
✓ Generating light with items such as candles or oil
✓ Clearing fields and forests

Today, however, we use energy in additional complex ways. We use energy for:

✓ Transportation
✓ Lighting
✓ Heating homes
✓ Food safety with refrigeration (fridges)
✓ Communication (telephones, television, and computers)
✓ Agriculture
✓ Increasing food productivity via nitrogen

All of the energy we use is generated from basically a few sources with the US pattern looking as follows:

Renewable Energy Consumption in the Nation's Energy Supply, 2008

Table 35

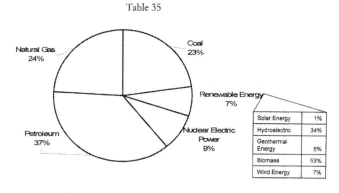

Solar Energy	1%
Hydroelectric	34%
Geothermal Energy	5%
Biomass	53%
Wind Energy	7%

Natural Gas 24%
Coal 23%
Renewable Energy 7%
Nuclear Electric Power 9%
Petroleum 37%

Source: US Energy Information Administration, Office of Coal, Nuclear, Electric and Alternate Fuels Chart data

Table 36

Fuel Used for Transportation, 2007

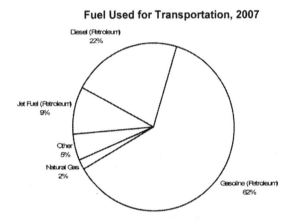

Note: Due to rounding, data may not sum to exactly 100%.
Source: U.S. Department of Energy, *Transportation Energy*
Data Book Edition **28 (2009)**

While I am not a peak oil theorist, the data peak oil theorists provide and that of conventional sources such as they IEA appear to be converging. The key information is the government-estimated, proven reserves, which are estimates of the recoverable oil from known sources under current operating processes. "Total global proved reserves have been estimated at approximately 1 trillion barrels since the late 1980s, because additions to reserves from new discoveries and from revisions to previous estimates have approximately matched the annual volume of oil produced (or withdrawn)."[147]

Oil is a complicated subject, as so many of the estimates are reliant on countries whose interests are best served by not revealing what their actual reserves are, while at the same time selling as much as they can. While presently we have seen declines in oil output from many major fields, the wars with Iraq have removed them as a player on the world market, and their production dropped from leading OPEC to thirteenth place. Now, Iraq, with the aid of international oil companies, wants to go from thirteenth place at 2.5m barrels a day to 13m barrels a day, a number that exceeds Saudi Arabia's output by 30 percent.[148] As you can expect, such a change in perspective and the willingness of oil companies to aid them for minimal profit can only drop world prices at a time when the United States needs it to bring back the economy. However, the question will be for how long Iraq will be able to sustain this, and whether this is good for everyone in the long term rather than nursing the resource until it is required. Regardless of the increase in oil exports from Iraq, we face a major problem.

Easy Oil

Oil is a substance extracted from below the earth's surface--not in large tanks but from oil-soaked pores and factures in the earth. During mining, there is an initial expansion of the oil that forces from the earth about 10 to 15 percent of the available oil. There are three stages to oil recovery:

> Primary recovery—up to 15 percent
> Secondary recovery—20 to 40 percent
> Tertiary recovery—up to 60 percent

The use of oil changes as prices are adjusted, with high prices being in the $200 per barrel range. However, these are conservative numbers in the estimate of some economists such as Jeff Rubin, who predicts $7 per gallon gasoline and $2 per liter pricing in line with Europe.[149]

Marion King Hubbert announced in 1949 that fossil fuels were running out. Born in Texas in 1903, Hubbert had degrees and advanced degrees, including his PHD from the University of Chicago. Then, after working in geological survey, he joined Shell Oil Company, where he was in charge of the research laboratory. A leading geologist, Hubbert had a number of scientific achievements. However, not content to rest, he continued to work and used statistical methods to predict the peak oil for US production between 1966 and 1972.

Hubbert was very close in his prediction, as the actual peak occurred in 1970. Peak oil theory has now become famous, and you can check out many Web sites that focus on identifying when peak oil has occurred in different countries. Peak oil is the point at which less oil is being pumped after the high point has been reached. Using data, Hubbert shows that oil production follows a curve in which rapid development of an oil field takes place. At some point, however, the oil that remains is more difficult to access. Using the same techniques but different data, Hubbert then predicted the global oil peak, although in this case with insufficient information he got the number wrong. Other researchers, however, have worked to refine and redo Hubbert's measures using better data. These include Colin J. Campbell, a geologist who worked for Amoco, who created the Association for the Study of Peak Oil, and who is also the author of *The Coming Oil Crisis*. There are many other people who support the peak oil theory, including those identified below:

> Richard Heinberg—*The Party's Over*
> Jeff Rubin—*Why Your World Is About to Get a Whole Lot Smaller*
> Kenneth S. Deffeyes—*Hubbert's Peak: The Impending World Oil Shortage*
> Walter Younquist—*GeoDestinies: The Inevitable Control of Earth Resources over Nations and Individuals*

Counter arguments against peak oil include:

> Peter Huber—Hard Green: Saving the Environment from the Environmentalists (1999)
> Bjorn Lomberg—*The Skeptical Environmentalist* (2001)

To understand oil consumption, you need to understand the global oil consumption patterns to see how these items relate. Table 37 and 38 from the IEO 2009 show consumption until 2030 for Organization of Economic Cooperation and Development (OECD) countries and for Non-OECD countries. If you add up the consumption and map it against the one trillion in proved resources by 2030, we are facing a drastic global challenge in easily accessible oil resources. The result will be a world where fuel costs in North America are in line with Europe now and Europe's costs have increased. In the last twenty-eight years, US oil production has decreased by 28 percent, while at the same time oil consumption has increased. The charts from government agencies all show that global demand is up and continues to increase significantly in non-OECD countries which are developing, as driven by purchases from the West.

This perspective can be mitigated in the view of Leonardo Maugeri, who believes that by 2030, thanks to new technologies our ability to extract oil will increase to up to 50 percent of a field versus the present average of 35 percent.[150] The example used in the magazine is the Kern River Oil Field, which started pumping in 1899. It initially was thought only 10 percent of its production could be extracted and yet so far extraction continues, though at a declined rate. His point is that past models of decline have, in his opinion, not proven correct in terms of the year predicted for peak and that increases in extraction technology will lead to tapping oil in once inaccessible areas. However, he does admit that oil production in the United States is on the decline, as the proven reserves are now 29 billion barrels. In the same article, he comments that

> Although oil and other fossil fuels pose risks for the climate and the environment, for now alternative sources cannot compare with their versatility, cost and ease of transport and storage. As the search continues we will need to be sure we use the oil we have responsibility.[151]

The world energy outlook, according to the IEA 2009 report, is that we will face a drop by almost two-thirds in existing fields by 2030 and that exploration will need intense investment. The natural gas forecast "is that additional capacity of around 2 700 bcm, or 4 times current Russian capacity, is needed by 2030—half to offset decline at existing fields and half to meet the increase in demand."[152] Such capacity does not exist today anywhere on the planet. The report is a dire prediction and factors in the demand for oil in non-OECD counties. However, oil consumption will not go down unless we take steps today. In addition, given the impact of Hurricane Katrina on the US oil fields and the increase in hurricanes, there will be an impact in North America on fuel prices, as so much of the US fuel supply is in hurricane-accessible areas—40 percent of the US refinery capacity is located in the Gulf of Mexico.[153] Additionally, deep-sea production peaks at a faster rate than land-based production, so oil fields in the Gulf of Mexico and in the other areas that we are drilling, which are smaller fields, have a shorter life for less of an economic payback. Oil fields all over the world are facing challenges to maintain supply. The largest field, Ghawar in Saudi Arabia, was discovered in 1948. The theory that oil supply will increase based on supply and demand is increasingly shown to be erroneous, even by those who believe the idea. Jeff Rubin who was Chief Economist at CIBC, points out, as do many economists, that the theory that supply will increase because demand increases is erroneous when you are dealing with a product of which there is a finite amount. Increasing demand for a finite resource cannot increase the amount of the resource you can access; all that will do is shift production to an alternative resource if one is available. This is what has happened with easy oil as demand has increased and supply has become more restricted—production has increased in alternative energies to offset this.

The Tar sands in Canada, Venezuela and the US are among the few places where we have a viable alternative, the oil sands have started to be utilized at an incredible rate in Canada, although to extract this fuel from the ground is a major consumer of other limited resources, such as water. In Utah alone the oil sands are estimated by the Utah Mining Association to contain 20-32 billion barrels of oil, although only one to two small scale projects have started. In Canada oil sands are in large scale development mode although to get at the oil in the tar sands the industry has to extract the sands using open-pit mining and then process it with water. The raw material is made up of bitumen, sand, and water. The first explorations of the sands started in 1906, when Von Hammerstein tried to find if there was oil under the sands. The Alberta Energy and Utilities Board believes the oil sands contain approximately 1.7 trillion barrels of bitumen, of which over 175 billion are recoverable with current technology, and 315 billion barrels with technological development.[154] Most of the oil sands are too deep for open-pit mining, so *in situ* techniques are used. This requires drilling and the injection of steam to heat the oil. The hot, thinner bitumen flows into wells, bringing it to the surface while the sand is left. This type of extraction method is expensive and requires a water source. In addition, the energy to extract this oil and the CO_2 emissions are higher—12.3 kilograms of CO_2 per a gallon versus 10.22 from primary oil and 23.15 for diesel extracted from coal.[155]

As you can see from Table 37 and Table 38 below, oil use in the developing non-OECD world is set to increase significantly while use in the OECD world does not decrease. Given this, unless we can extract more oil from existing wells, as Maugeri suggested, we will be limited in our ability to extract oil. Directionally, many can argue that there is no crisis. However, the words they speak are not in line with their actions. Why are major players investing billions in oil sand plants in Canada to extract inherently more expensive oil made from bitumen when they could extract oil much more easily from conventional wells? The reasons are twofold—the fact that conventional, large-scale wells on the order of the wells in Saudi Arabia have not been found for a long time and also that more and more countries where oil exist at even marginal levels are nationalizing to control a greater share of their domestic resource. Many countries take a high percentage of the revenue oil companies receive, while in a few limited places, such as Canada where the government supports market forces, there is very little chance of nationalization although oil companies pay minimal amounts to the government. The challenge of getting at diminishing resources means the United States needs not only Canadian oil, of which it is a top importer, but must also develop extensive Gulf of Mexico resources. Development of these new deepwater wells have slowed now due to lower prices but also due to the impact of Hurricane Katrina on the oil industry and the political consequence of the Gulf of Mexico oil spill. Deepwater wells, which have to go 1,000 to 5,000 (ultra deepwater) meters deep, cost hundreds of millions of dollars to drill and pose a significant environmental risk if companies do not Environmentally Proof their business against the risk of equipment and process failure. The deepwater Gulf of Mexico region has far fewer wells drilled and accompanying exploration data than areas closer to shore, making it more difficult to predict where the largest pockets of oil and gas might lie.[156] However, Gulf oil and Mexico provides 70 percent of the oil and 36 percent of the natural oil in the area.[157] Oil companies would need 139 deepwater production platforms for their plans to occur, a *Scientific American* article states.[158] Minimal contracts for platform development have been awarded, and additional potential production for 2011 has been cut by 2.4 million barrels of oil a day.

The rate of return for any energy extracted from other sources aside from oil, which is the lowest extract cost, is important. So, to extract oil from tar or shale or even the deep sea requires a higher cost for extraction than easy oil. If the price of oil is too low, it does not make sense to extract oil from additional sources, which is why when the price of oil surged in 2008, the amount of investment into the Canadian oil sands grew dramatically. Equally intense was the fall in the value of the oil sands projects and the number cancelled when the price per barrel of oil went to $40. Only with the resurgence of oil prices to the $70 to $80-range, was continuing project development and extraction of the oil really profitable. The cost of extraction in the oil sands includes the cost of the natural gas that must be burned to heat the water for the in situ extraction process. As Jeff Rubin points out, for Canada to increase oil sands production to four million barrels per day, "Canada would have to cannibalize its natural gas exports to the United States to do it."[159]

Presently, oil companies are looking for alternative sources of fuel. However, there are no oil sources presently available to replace what we have found. We can, as said before, increase extraction from the existing wells, though that requires energy to do. Reading the announcement mentioned before from the IEA makes you wonder why so many people remain ignorant of what is taking place. The reality is that some of the largest companies are planning for fuel price increases, and even as they develop these plans, they do not notify the population. They also do not have a set plan—no one is trying to put out the fire aside from those who are motivated to try to reduce their carbon footprint, which, if you think about it, is completely connected to reducing oil use. Reduce carbon use and you reduce fuel use as the carbon that is being created is coming from the fuel that is being burned. More and more oil companies are searching in the most remote parts of the earth and making deals with countries such as Iraq because they have no choice.

We need to make clear that we cannot stop the increasing industrialization and growth of oil consumption in the developing countries without the risk of war. Countries such as China and India and many others with high rates of poverty will not stand by while the West continues to grow and consume a rate of energy use way in excess of the population while leaving the rest of the world in poverty. The very countries from which we buy oil are increasing users of the very resource they are selling. Many of these countries, such as Saudi Arabia, power their grid with oil, which is a very expensive proposition. They also have now become users of air conditioners and expensive cars that are high consumers of fuel. In many oil-producing countries, oil is subsidized so that there is no market mechanism forcing people, due to higher prices, to adjust and reduce their consumption. In addition, in China and India, while their consumption is increasing, their level of consumption per capita is very low relative to that of the OECD and the United States and Canada in particular. The energy use in these areas is also growing as we continue to shift production there so that companies can take advantage not only of the cheaper labor but the lower oil prices.

However, at the same time, if the developed countries continue to buy low-value (value in terms of quality, sustainability, and product life) products from these areas, we will only continue to devastate the world environment. People in China and poor countries do not have a vast care about the United States and its needs—their concerns are living daily and having their own needs met. At the same time, we need to examine if as governments and companies we should be exporting the resource-rich consumer lifestyle of the West that we know we ourselves cannot support. As a doctor friend of ours told me recently, she believes the world could support billons more if the West was willing to adjust its lifestyle. People in the west consume at times more than 18% above their daily required intake. We drive large cars to work when we could have one small car that consumed half of what we presently use. At the same time, an immediate drop in consumption would have a significant impact on the West as the stability of the entire Middle East, which has a young, volatile population, is dependent on oil revenue. A sudden drop in buying could have the same impact on the Muslim world and OPEC nations such as Venezuela as the embargo of Cuba has had. We need energy and a political and environmental solution that is time phased to allow for cultural and civilian adjustments, and yet we need one which recognizes that oil is in decline. The following two charts show oil usage in 2010 and the projected numbers by the US Energy Department for 2030.

Table 37 & Table 38
World Liquids Consumption by Region, Reference Case, 1990-2030
(Million Barrels per Day)

Region/Country	History	Projections						
	1990	2005	2006	2010	2015	2020	2025	2030
OECD North America	20.5	25.2	25.1	23.5	24.1	24.4	25.2	26.2
United States /a	17.0	20.8	20.7	19.6	20.2	20.2	20.8	21.7
Canada	1.7	2.3	2.3	2.3	2.3	2.3	2.4	2.5
Mexico	1.8	2.1	2.1	1.5	1.7	1.9	2.0	2.1
OECD Europe	13.7	15.7	15.7	14.5	14.5	14.9	15.0	15.0
OECD Asia	7.2	8.6	8.5	8.4	8.6	8.8	8.8	8.7
Japan	5.3	5.3	5.2	4.6	4.8	5.0	4.8	4.7
South Korea	1.0	2.2	2.2	2.8	2.7	2.6	2.7	2.8
Australia/New Zealand	0.8	1.1	1.1	1.0	1.1	1.2	1.2	1.3
Total OECD	41.4	49.5	49.2	46.3	47.2	48.1	48.9	50.0
Non-OECD								
Non-OECD Europe and Eurasia	9.4	4.9	5.0	5.1	5.2	5.4	5.4	5.5
Russia	5.4	2.8	2.8	2.7	2.8	2.9	2.8	2.7
Other	3.9	2.1	2.1	2.4	2.4	2.5	2.6	2.7
Non-OECD Asia	6.6	15.3	16.0	17.8	20.6	24.2	27.3	30.2
China	2.3	6.7	7.2	8.5	10.0	12.1	13.8	15.3
India	1.2	2.5	2.7	2.4	3.1	3.9	4.3	4.7
Other Non-OECD Asia	3.1	6.1	6.1	6.9	7.5	8.2	9.1	10.2
Middle East	3.5	5.8	6.1	7.0	7.4	7.9	8.5	9.4
Africa	2.1	3.0	3.0	3.5	3.6	3.7	3.8	3.9
Central and South America	3.8	5.5	5.7	6.6	6.6	6.8	7.1	7.6
Brazil	1.5	2.2	2.3	2.5	2.8	3.0	3.4	3.7
Other Central and South America	2.3	3.3	3.4	4.0	3.8	3.7	3.8	3.9
Total Non-OECD	25.3	34.5	35.8	40.0	43.4	47.8	52.2	56.6
Total World	66.7	84.0	85.0	86.3	90.6	95.9	101.1	106.6

Sources: History: Energy Information Administration (EIA), International Energy Annual 2006 (June-December 2008), web site www.eia.doe.gov/iea. Projections: EIA, Annual Energy Outlook 2009, DOE/EIA-0383(2009) (Washington, DC, March 2009), AEO2009 National Energy Modeling System, run AEO2009.D120908A, web site www.eia.doe.gov/oiaf/aeo; and World Energy Projections Plus (2009).

As you can see from the charts above, even when China or India increases their energy use, the United States will still, with a much smaller population, be using 25 percent of the world's oil. This is not sustainable. If we looked on the world as a business and the energy use of the United States as an expense and that of China as revenue, the United States and OECD needs to stop running us into debt. However, this means that everyone in OECD countries would need to accept a lower standard of living. The non-OECD countries would then be able to increase their oil consumption per capita without affecting the overall global requirement. However, as we can see with the recent economic issues, no one wants to change their consumption patterns. Instead, everyone wants more which is how we got into the economic crisis we are in, whether you see it as oil-price driven, increases in the price of energy correlated with economic issues, or driven by the sub-prime mortgages.

Looking at the sources of energy below shows you that the United States needs to come to grips with its oil consumption due to the world's inability to sustain the global demand, of which the United States is 25 percent, and also with the security issues that will increasing take place. A change in president, as occurred in Venezuela, had a impact on their supplying the United States, so politics is a key oil supply determinate. The only country that the United States can relay on for oil supply in which it does not have troops directly is Canada. This section should have provided you with enough information to be able to understand that the end of easy oil is at hand and all the other choices have significant trade-offs.

In terms of the United States, below is US energy information showing the top sources of petroleum to the United States.

Table 39

Total Imports of Petroleum (Top 15 Countries)
(Thousand Barrels per Day)

Country	Nov-09	Oct-09	YTD 2009	Nov-08	YTD 2008
CANADA	2,527	2,363	2,447	2,534	2,482
MEXICO	1,083	1,136	1,237	1,406	1,308
VENEZUELA	890	955	1,099	1,236	1,191
SAUDI ARABIA	848	943	1,023	1,514	1,535
NIGERIA	980	869	783	827	993
IRAQ	458	499	461	476	636
ALGERIA	400	491	483	677	554
ANGOLA	431	450	477	450	509
RUSSIA	425	385	570	445	473
COLOMBIA	237	292	282	176	201
UNITED KINGDOM	190	278	249	245	242
VIRGIN ISLANDS	205	215	275	338	323
ECUADOR	155	180	187	229	217
BRAZIL	268	174	319	286	261
AZERBAIJAN	74	134	69	71	74

Note: The data in the table above excludes oil imports into US territories.

Source: US Energy Information Administration (Nov 2008).

Canada as shown is the number one exporter of oil to the United States, all other states that the United States and the world buy from have significant political risks or their own oil needs such as the UK this is the reason growth in oil sands production is important. However at risk with increasing oil sands production is another key resource, water.

Trend 3 Fresh Water Crisis and Ocean Depletion

Fresh water is a subject that should be close to the stomach and heart of everyone, especially to businesspeople who make their living from food, restaurants, sports, oil production, and energy. Take your average hamburger, which requires 2,400 liters, or 630 gallons, of water to produce.[160] As the water shortage accelerates in combination with the food crisis, we will be eating a lot less of both. This means if your business does not prioritize, your main seller will evaporate, leaving you high and unprofitable. The human body is made up almost 60 percent water, and we need to drink water daily to replace the water we lose via perspiration and toilet functions, including urine. There are general recommendations that people should drink eight glasses of water a day, however, guidelines vary as different people consume varying calories and have varying activity levels. Water is used for almost all the activities we engage in:

- ✓ Providing water for personnel consumption
- ✓ Cooking
- ✓ Laundry
- ✓ Flushing toilets
- ✓ Washing and cleaning our bodies
- ✓ Sports (skating, skiing, swimming)
- ✓ Agricultural irrigation of plants and lawns
- ✓ Watering agricultural animals
- ✓ Recreational swimming
- ✓ Cooling power plants (nuclear, coal fired, cooling engines)
- ✓ Fish habitats
- ✓ Oil production

According to the World Bank, more then 1.1 billion people do not have access to safe fresh water, and 2.6 billion do not have access to basic sanitation. There is a project called the Millennium Project to address water. However, many of the issues affecting water are not restricted sub-Sahara Africa but now affect the United States and countries such as China. The driver behind the coming water crisis is the consumption pattern of the civilization that we have built, which requires intense water use to survive. The world is made up of mostly water. However, only 3 percent of the water on the earth is fresh—97 percent is salt water, which is undrinkable unless desalinated. The majority of the freshwater in the world resides in the United States and Canada, with the majority in Canada. However, major parts of the world are running out of water, including the Midwestern United States, China, Africa, the Middle East, and sections of South America.

This scarcity of water has often been written about by Maude Barlow in books such as *Blue Covenant*[161] and other books. While, as mentioned before, billions at the bottom of the pyramid do not have access to fresh water, we will focus on the key areas that are critical to business development while not denying that we need to aid and help those much less fortunate than ourselves.

The crisis in water first came to my attention when working on the management group for a division of one of the world's largest farming co-ops. The question arose as to what would happen to cheese prices in a few years. In this meeting there where graphs, charts, and many numbers, but the core fact that I went away with was that the massive drought that Australia had been experiencing for a few years had reached the point that it had affected their dairy farming industry, and this was driving a price increase. Now, this was not looked on as a positive, but neither was it a negative. From a business perspective, higher world prices were a positive in the short term. However, from a consumer perspective, it was a negative, as this was affecting the prices of the milk powder industry, driving prices higher for many in poor, developing countries. In the world's perspective, what this did was shift milk manufacturing to countries in the north and increase the milk price. But in ten to fifteen years, if droughts continue in Australia and spread, then many of our consumers and workers and the generations of people we will depend on to be creative and get us out of this crisis will be affected, as many will be unable to afford a proper regime of milk. Poorer consumers means less effective workers and thinkers in a changed economy where countries' prosperity is linked no longer to just manual labor but to the innovative and creative nature of their population.

The point is as a business you need to look at how these broad trends will play out. Yesterday, the drought in Australia was a positive, but if that extends to the United States, such a drought will go from a positive for North America to a very fast negative. Some key statistics follow.

Key Water and Sanitation Statistics

Water withdrawals for irrigation have increased by over 60 percent since 1960. About 70 percent of all available fresh water is used for irrigation in agriculture. Yet, because of inefficient irrigation systems, particularly in developing countries, 60 percent of this water is lost to evaporation or is returned to rivers and groundwater aquifers (UN-WWAP, 2006: 173).

Water use increased six-fold during the twentieth century, more than twice the rate of population growth. While water consumption in industrialized countries runs as high as 380 liters per capita per day in the United States (USGS, 2004) and 129 liters/capita/day in Germany, (Statistisches Bundesamt, 2000), in developing countries 20–30 liters/capita/day are considered enough to meet basic human needs.

In parts of the United States, China, and India, groundwater is being consumed faster than it is being replenished, and groundwater tables are steadily falling. Some rivers, such as the Colorado River in the western United States and the Yellow River in China, often run dry before they reach the sea.

Freshwater ecosystems have been severely degraded. It is estimated that about half the world's wetlands have been lost, and more than 20 percent of the world's 10,000 known freshwater species have become extinct, threatened, or endangered (UN-DESA: 10).

The Global Water Supply Situation

Up to 30 percent of freshwater supplies are lost due to leakage in developed countries, and in some major cities, losses can run as high as 40 to 70 percent (UN-WWAP, 2006: 150).

Water, Sanitation, and Health

Every week, an estimated 42,000 people die from diseases related to low-quality drinking water and lack of sanitation. Over 90 percent of them are children under the age of five (WHO/UNICEF, 2005: 15).

Two of the water-related diseases, diarrhea and malaria, ranked third and fourth place in the cause of death among children under five years old, accounting for 17 percent and 8 percent, respectively, of all deaths (WHO, 2005: 106).

United States

Water use in the United States is one of the highest in the world, at 100 gallons a day. This much water also requires energy to move, purify, and access via purification systems and pumps. Energy is the most significant user of water in the United States. Water is also required for agricultural food growth. Lake Lanier is a prime example of the impact that a water shortage can have on a city. The lake's water supply dried up due to overuse as the population has increased. The key issue here is partly, as it is everywhere, an increase in population without clear freshwater management and control. According to the U.S. Geological Survey, the US uses

410,000 million gallons per day (Mgal/d) of water as of 2005. About 80 percent of the total (328,000 Mgal/d) withdrawal was from surface water, and about 82 percent of the surface water withdrawn was freshwater. The remaining 20 percent (82,600 Mgal/d) was withdrawn from groundwater, of which about 96 percent was freshwater. If withdrawals for thermoelectric power in 2005 are excluded, withdrawals were 210,000 Mgal/d, of which 129,000 Mgal/d (62 percent) was supplied by surface water and 80,700 Mgal/d (38 percent) was supplied by groundwater. Water withdrawals in four states—California, Texas, Idaho, and Florida—accounted for more than one-fourth of all fresh and saline water withdrawn in the United States in 2005. More than half (53 percent) of the total withdrawals of 45,700 Mgal/d in California were for irrigation, and 28 percent were for thermoelectric power. Most of the withdrawals in Texas (26,700 Mgal/d) were for thermoelectric power (43 percent) and irrigation (29 percent). Irrigation accounted for 85 percent of the 19,500 Mgal/d of water withdrawn in Idaho, and thermoelectric power accounted for 66 percent of the 18,300 Mgal/d withdrawn in Florida.[162]

Production of energy in the United States uses massive amounts of energy, as it does in Canada—especially in Alberta for the oil sands. To quench the need for water as the construction of surface reservoirs have slowed in the United States, there has been an increasing use of ground water from aquifers.[163] These semi-renewable resources can replenish if given the right resources. However, the majority have not been adequately replenished due to the changes in infrastructure in areas surrounding and covering them. In addition, pollution is creating a case where getting clean, fresh water is an issue.

A *New York Times* investigation of water pollution records[164] showed the Clean Water Act was violated more than 506,000 times since 2004, by more than 23,000 companies and other facilities, according to reports submitted by polluters themselves. Violations ranged from failing to report emissions to dumping toxins at levels that might contribute to illnesses. The vast majority of those polluters escaped punishment (visit www.nytimes.com/toxicwaters). In addition, The *Times* interviewed more than 250 state and federal regulators, water system managers, environmental advocates, and scientists. That research showed an estimated one in ten Americans was exposed to drinking water failing to meet federal requirements. The pollution of water, along with access to fresh water, is a problem. Susan Marks[165] compiled a list of access issues of which we have extracted and a few are shown below:

- ✓ 2007 was the driest year on record for North Carolina in 113 years
- ✓ New Hampshire's aquifer contamination
- ✓ Kentucky water issues due to the cessation of water flow in the Licking River
- ✓ Tennessee water issues in 2008 and a number of other states due to a lack of rainfall
- ✓ Water capacity issues in Alabama
- ✓ California droughts

The United States is far from a safe water environment. Now let's look at the opposite side of the world, China. Southern China and the Shanghai area, as we discussed before, have become the manufacturing plant of the world. This has driven a massive increase in water utilization as the population has shifted from being dispersed across the country to concentrate into large cities due to the massive increase in production capacity. In 2003, 38.1 percent of China's rivers were considered polluted, and the water quality has continued to drop. Fifty percent of the pollution comes from nutrient runoff, pesticides—China is one of the largest pesticide users in the world—emissions from intensive livestock production, and industrial and municipal wastewater discharges and solid wastes make up the rest.[166] Water scarcity has affected north of the Yangtze River, and across the country, shortages are growing in number. For all increasing areas, it is affecting the economy. In 2000, shortages were calculated at 38.8 billion cbm and projected to be 56.5 billion cbm by 2050. A World Bank study estimated the cost to the Chinese economy of between US$620 million and US$1.06 billion. Draining aquifers to provide the water has resulted in land subsidence in cities and saltwater intrusion along the coast, depleting groundwater and aquifers. The draining of aquifers is contributing to drought and dust storms and creating urban refugees. The water shortage will also affect China's ability, as it will in the United States, to produce electricity, oil, and food.

Oceans

Not only is fresh water an issue, but so is ocean water, as the oceans experience dead zones where nothing lives, such as in Chesapeake Bay. One zone is as big as 17,000 square kilometers, and it has doubled in size since its discovery.[167]

Trend 4 Population Growth

The world's population is forecasted to be nine billion by 2050. This is true even after adjusting for the decline in the birthrate that has happened in the first half of the twentieth century. Birthrates have declined in Western countries, and they have slowed globally. This will not, however, prevent the world's population from increasing to the level of nine billion. After we achieve this high number, the population will drop. Unfortunately, the world cannot, given poor present consumption patterns, sustain populations much above our present levels without significant changes in way we do business. Nine billion people, given climate change, the end of easy oil, water depletion, and our present technological basis is not achievable, much less sustainable. To get to even nine billion means the people at the bottom of the pyramid will increase dramatically. People in the rest of the world will not sit by while Western countries, defined as the United States, Canada, Australia, New Zealand, and Western European countries, and the Asian tigers and Japan continue to be wealthy while they move further into poverty. Even China, with its focus on growing its economy, cannot continue to achieve high growth rates longer term if it does not focus on the issues identified, and the food concerns we will soon discuss.

While population predictions do have errors based on migration, fertility, life span, disease vectors,[168] and changes in culture, the fact remains that the world's population is set to change significantly. In sixteen years, the world's population will be eight billion people; this is a significant increase of 1.3 billion over the estimate at present. This growth means that world resources will be taxed. At the same time, immigration will need to increase in Western countries to compensation for the decline in the birthrate of the European-descended population. What we are seeing is the coloring of the world as the world is transformed from a homogenous color chart, depending on location, to an increasing mix over the next decades as birthrates of families with European origins decline and migration and migrants' relatively higher birthrates take hold. Politically, we have already seen what long-term trends in these countries can do politically with the election of President Obama.

This increase in population will come at the same time as family sizes decrease. In 1970, women had an average of 4.5 children. In 2000, women had an average of 2.7 children. This is just above the 2.1 level needed for a stable population. Regardless of the drop in growth, however, the population of the world will still increase, and this poses a tremendous challenge and opportunity.

The chart below shows past world population data back to year one and future world population projections through the year 2050.

Table 40

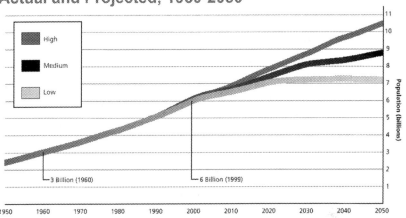

Source: United Nations. 1998. *World Population Prospects (1998 The Revision).*

Not only will world resources be taxed by the population increase, but countries' resources will be disproportionably affected since the most growth will be in countries that already struggle to support existing growth due to geographic and environment challenges (see Appendix A). The top ten countries for growth have in the majority a desert-type environment with very little arable land. Since this growth is also in Middle Eastern or countries on which we depend for oil, these countries will start to consume a larger percentage of the oil they presently export, reducing the amount available for export. In addition, they will require a higher return on their exported resources, or they will be unable to offset the growth with employment. The increase in the population size and the change to younger populations means these countries will be more unstable while they face greater internal challenges from jihad Islamists with their borders. Countries with younger populations tend to be inherently more unstable, as the younger people call for change in the middle of higher unemployment.

The higher population growth will drive a need for incremental housing and for resources that are already limited. Housing demand will increase in southern countries, where land for agriculture is already at a premium. Population shifts will drive a massive reallocation of resources and changes in export patterns as the population in Western Hemisphere ages and demand for goods such as toys and clothes decrease while the demand for these items increase in other countries.

Poverty will increase as the population increases. World Bank estimates show about 1.4 billion people presently living below the international poverty line of US$1.25 a day in 2005—equivalent to more than one-fourth of the developing world's population. Poverty incidence declined from 52 percent of the global population in 1981 to 42 percent in 1990 and 25 percent in 2005. However, a definition of $1.25 a day is not recognizing the gravity of the situation when it takes 1500 calories a day minimum to feed each person and prevent starvation. Population is a key part of the issues we face and is a multiplier of the impact we need to address as business leaders.

The increase in population is a challenge but also an opportunity, as each new mouth will need to be fed and each body clothed. Population, like all the changes we face, is a great opportunity for companies to drive profitability while servicing their customers if we move away from a cheap, disposable mentality to one where we build products and services that will last. If we build value-added, long-lasting products, recycling and reuse will mean something and we can increase the welfare of many. If, however, we continue to use the present capitalist model of cheap, we will not be able to feed and clothe the population. What we need is a true consumerism-based capitalist society in which consumer workers know the value of items and can make a true selection of value for a product, like shoes that will last them a lifetime but may cost more rather than twenty pairs that consumes resources and end in the garbage. Our drive to buy and replace new with new needs to shift to buying new and reusing and recycling. Focusing on this, along with living a healthier lifestyle, will make a huge difference in North America and the West as we consume 18 percent more calories than we need on average. If we apply these calories in the right place, we could drastically reduce hunger, but only if we stop promoting the cheap, unsustainable lifestyle that so many companies promote. We need to ensure we do not develop marketing plans for products that will make a short-term profit but have a significant long-term impact, and this is no truer than in the area of food.

Trend 5 Food Crisis

Given a rising population, we will require the equivalent of another 2.1 billion acres of arable land to feed this population increase, which is the equivalent of an area the size of Brazil.[169] If you review the numbers below, by approximately 2025 the earth will have a population of over eight billion people, even with the projected decrease in growth levels. All of these people will need to be fed.

TABLE 41

World Population Growth[2]:1950-2050

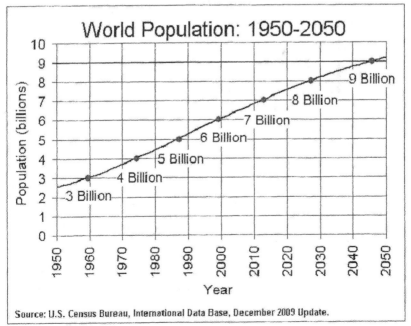

Source: U.S. Census Bureau, International Data Base, December 2009 Update.

This increase means we will need to review what types of food we produce and where and how we sell this food. The food industry itself will have to change. The impact of large-scale production will need to be reviewed, as so much of our food now is produced on large-scale farms requiring massive amounts of pesticide and fertilizer that pollutes the water tables and contributes to unsafe water conditions. We will also need to adjust the level of protein consumption. To truly understand the impact food will have, an excellent and fascinating read is *The End of Food* by Paul Roberts.

The history of food is important, as we can see historically what will happen as populations increase while land areas decrease. Thomas Malthus first proposed, in his 1798 "Principle of Population," that food production could only increase arithmetically, while population would increase geometrically. Malthus proposed that population would exceed food production at some point and global starvation would occur.

Population growth has taken place in keeping with his theory, although the rate of growth has slowed. In terms of food production, however, the conversion of land in North and South America dedicated to agricultural production and the agricultural revolution enabled global food production to increase. Over the 209-year span since 1700, farmers dramatically improved their ability to produce food, especially the amount of meat. Before this period, soil health was maintained by allowing land to lie fallow for a year and by utilizing crop rotation to replace lost nitrogen. At the same time, legislation in Europe resulted in peasants losing land rights, which were then taken over by the nobility, who absorbed the peasants' small lots. This facilitated large migrations to land in North and South America and other British colonies. The merger of small farms into larger ones in Europe and the growth of large farms in the western hemispheres using territory from which indigenous people had been moved to reservations or vacated due to disease, resulted in farms of a size that had never been seen before in any other countries. In Canada, farms were large but not of the size they would grow to with the invention of machinery-based farming using combines and other large farm equipment.

Increased irrigation from aquifers in the Southwestern United States also caused large areas that had never been cultivated before to be transformed into farmland. Almost more important than the invention of the steam engine was the revolution in farming implements, from the cotton ginner by Eli Whitney in 1793, to the harvester by Cyrus McCormick in 1834, to John Deere's invention in 1837 of the cast-steel plow with a steel share. Where the tool could not be adjusted to the crop, breeding quickly allowed the crop to be adjusted to the tool. Starting in the twentieth century, scientists focused on what breeding plants and genetically modifying what plants could be farmed where while increasing yield. Increased corn production using cross breeding produced yields of 20 to 25 percent larger crops on fewer acres. Plant breeding was also applied to wheat and maize to increase the yield of both crops, allowing farmers to feed a hungry world. US farms have become large, as shown in the data below. Farms of greater than 1,000 acres increased by 14 percent between 1982 and 2002, and those of 50–1,000 acres declined by about 17 percent. Small farms of less than 50 acres are less than 2 percent of all farmland in 2002, while those greater than 1,000 acres represented two-thirds of all farms.[171] This continuing increase in farm size is only possible due to the increased use of farm machinery which is dependent on oil.

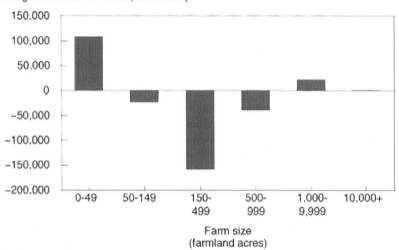

More large farms, more very small farms, fewer in the middle

Change in number of farms (1982-2002)

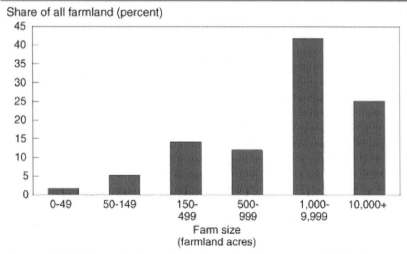

Most farmland is in large farming operations, 2002

Share of all farmland (percent)

Source: USDA, Economic Research Service tabulations based on USDA, National Agricultural Statistics Service's Census of Agriculture data.

Table 42

Breeding and planting of fields with a monoculture resulted in the ability to farm more effectively. However, crop rotation impacted farming effectiveness until the addition of fertilizer and pesticides, starting with DDT. Fertilizers come largely in the form of nitrogen. Fritz Haber, a German scientist, received the Nobel Prize in 1919 for his work on nitrogen fixing, using air with hydrogen derived mainly from natural gas (methane) to create ammonia.

Beef

Cattle have long been a staple of civilization, and in the eighteenth and nineteenth centuries, increasing farmers increasingly experimented with different types of cattle. At the same time, Louis Pasteur's discovery of pasteurization created new ways to move milk aside from the long-utilized ways of butter and cheese. This supported the change in the breeding of cattle so that now milk could be stored and transported further. The increase in speed with rail and the invention of refrigeration increased our ability to distribute milk products. Now farmers could get the benefit of breeding cows that could produce vast quantities of milk. At the same time, a large cow meant people could consume more beef. For example, where a cow at one time was 350 pounds, calves now mass at 475 pounds and are mature at 1375 pounds. From 1975 to 2005, cows' weights have increased by 200 pounds.[172] The increases in farm size and cattle size resulted in increased food consumption. However, this is not sustainable given the increase in the world's population. At a time when we need to start focusing on food products that are less resource intensive, the US meat industry has driven a global fascination with meat.

> Consumption of meat in the U.S. is 124 kg/capita/y, compared to the global average of 38 kg. The countries that consume the least amount of meat are in Africa and South Asia; the lowest ten are Sierra Leone, Democratic Republic of Congo, Mozambique, Sri Lanka, Rwanda, India, Malawi, Guinea, Burundi and Bangladesh.

Consumption in these countries is between 3 and 5 kg/capita/y. This is compensated to some extent in Bangladesh by higher fish consumption (17.5 kg) and in India and Sri Lanka by higher milk consumption (47.5 kg and 35.9 kg, respectively). Milk consumption in the U.S. is 118 kg/capita/y.[173]

The problem with this level of meat consumption, regardless of the efficiencies of the conversion of chickens and pork versus cows, is less than 3kg of grain are required to produce 1 kg of meat on an average basis.[174] We do not have enough grain to feed the population if such large amounts of grain are removed from the food cycle to feed second-source protein producers and generate biofuels. Some studies including one by Biofuels, which found that

> The U.S. increased corn production by 157 million tonnes of corn since 1995. 31 million net tonnes of grain went to support U.S. ethanol production, and 27 million tonnes supported a 15 percent increase in U.S. population during the period. By contrast, the study projected that livestock grain demand to supply Chinese meat consumption increased by 199 million tonnes between 1995 and 2007.
>
> This is a dramatic increase, although China's meat consumption is still 45 percent less than the average consumption in the U.S.

The Chinese consumer cannot increase meat consumption to the levels even close to those in North America, based on present production means, without significantly affecting the global agriculture industry. This means that if we want to prevent starvation on a massive scale, North American, European and global meat-eating habits will have to change as those grain stocks will be required to feed people in developing countries.[175] We can either change what we are doing or force starvation on the world on a massive level.

Our food problem, however, goes beyond that of the supply of food. It also concerns how we have genetically manipulated animals to become food animals. One summer I went for a trip to the United States and visited Smithfield, the town where Smithfield, the pork producer, raises millions of pigs. Just outside the Virginia town, there is a yacht club with a lighthouse you can sleep in, and yet the river the club was built on was so polluted you could not swim in it. You could smell the farm from there—it was an aroma like nothing you can imagine. The growth of US pig farming went largely unmonitored, and then in 1996 the earth wall of a lagoon broke, sending 22 million gallons of water and pig waste into a river above Jacksonville. Five other spills followed elsewhere. Emergency inspections by two state agencies after the June spill found 124 lagoons filled to the brim and 526 dangerously overloaded.[176] In the state of North Carolina, domestic animal waste is the largest contributor of river pollution. The hog industry of North Carolina, between 1986 and 2005, grew from 2.4 to 9.7 million hogs, which makes it rank second in terms of pig production in the United States. Swine are the largest contributors of pollution among domesticated animals in North Carolina. To address this farms need to use a treatment plant with solid-liquid separation.[177] Unsustainable agricultural techniques will affect our food supply at a critical time when they need to expand if we do not make changes today.

Chapter 10: Closing Summary

So, what does all this mean for your government or business? If you are in government we have identified concepts that on implementation will transform your environmental staunch so you can address the issues in an environmentally economically viable way. If you are managing in an international or global company, you will face increased stress as the trends continue and the economy relapses in another recession as it cannot support the stress we are placing on the planet. What should your business strategy be as the population that could afford your products faces increased poverty? Your strategy must focus on Environmental Proofing of your business and utilizing the Value Chain, Supply Chain and Logistics processes we have identified to reduce your costs and environmental footprint while building innovative solutions focused on addressing, the convenience and consumption gap; between our desires and what the planet can sustain. This is where Value profits and the tools we have described factor in. Your business needs to make a change now, selecting either option 3 or 4 below.

1. Do nothing, continuing our present ways of operating and hope the global outcome is favorable.
2. Try to stabilize our growth at present levels and hope the outcome is favorable.

3. Try to stabilize or control the climate and natural capital factors so we can control the impact as we grow.

4. Work to set the climate and natural capital environmental levels back to ones more conducive for people.

The answer is obvious, and so a few large businesses are reacting to the broads trends we face by developing sustainable business models. However, implementing these changes away from a Easy Profit driven world is dependent on growing your Value profits while at the same time implementing cost allocation adjustments to provide the funds required for innovative development.

We hope this book has given you a new perspective. The risks that unsustainable growth and Easy Profits are to the needs and wants of billions of people and millions of companies will drive change. Altering global resource consumption patterns will require the participation and involvement of consumers, workers, businesses, and governments, but it can be achieved. In this book, we have identified organizational strategies and tactics allowing you to achieve peak performance. These Business Culture, Value Chain, Operations, Supply Chain and Logistics strategies can be implemented with minimal risk if you have the political and organizational will, personnel motivation and empowered trained staff to apply them to your organization.

You should know we kept the information we could provide to a minimum to focus you on our mission of identifying actionable alternatives and processes that can drive cost reduction and improve sustainability. At the start, I mentioned that I developed strategies and led team to implement those strategies savings over $200 million. Those changes resulted in reduced waste and improved profit. This approach works, as business and government and consumers all want the same thing in the end—a world that their children can live and work in while creating value. While we did not cover job creation in detail, you should be able to see from the processes described that as we increase innovation and change, jobs will be created. We have not addressed some of the more often-sold plans to address energy needs, such as windmills and nuclear energy as our focus in on the drivers of consumption and management. Infrastructure ideas are often promoted however the reality is for the infrastructure to be built we will need to reduce our baseline consumption patterns if we are to have the resources to make such significant changes.

In addressing government and business cooperation, we need to look at models such as the US Metropolitan Planning Organizations (there are 385), which have worked on transportation strategy in US cities. If we can have similar sustainable environmental processes started in cities, which is where change needs to start, the partnership and planning of projects between business and government will allow for improvements. We will start to develop the democratic, citizen-driven participation with companies that, along with marketing and strategic business plans in business and government, can drive changes using Value Profitability processes. The key is realizing that we gain no profit if our branding states we are dedicated to helping others and at the end of the day, our planet and our brothers and sisters are naked and destitute of food.[178]

If you are interested in reducing your costs and increasing your value by implementing the ideas and concepts here, visit our website at www.AKCELLconsulting.com.

Bibliography

Baker, Susan. *New Consumer Marketing: Managing a Living Demand System.* New York: John Wiley & Sons, 2003.

Barlow, Maude. *Blue Covenant: The Global Water Crisis and the Coming Battle for the Right to Water.* Toronto: McClelland & Stewart Ltd., 2007.

Bedworth D. David and Bailey E. James, Integrated Production Control Systems, Management Analysis, Design, Wiley &Sons Inc, 1982 p. 88-130.

Berger L. Peter and Huntington P. Samuel, Many Globalizations, Oxford 2002

Boyer Karel Kenneth, Frohlich T. Markham and Hult Thomas G., Extending the Supply Chain, AMACON, 2005

Bradford D. Smart PH.D., Topgrading, Portfolio, 2005

Brugmann Jeb, Welcome to the Urban Revolution, Viking Canada 2009

Christensen M. Clayton, The Innovators Solution, HBS Press, 2003

Collins, Jim, Good to Great, Harper Business 2001

Cooper, G Robert, (Winning at New Products), 2001

Diamond Jared, Guns, Germs, and Steel, The Fates of Human Societes Norton, 1999, 1997

Dyer Gwynne, Climate Wars, Vintage Canada, 2008

Dunn Davis, Building The Brand Driven Business, Jossey-Bass, 2002

Estes Jonathan, Smart Green, How to Implement Sustainable Business Practises in Any Industry and Make Money, John Wily & Sons Inc. 2009

Finkelstein Sydney, Why Smart Executives Fail and what you can learn from their mistakes, Portfolio, 2003

Frazelle Edward, Supply Chain Strategy, The Logistics of Supply Chain Management, McGraw-Hill, 2002

Goleman Daniel, Ecological Intelligence, Broadway Books, 2009

Gore, Al, An Inconvenient Truth, Rodale, 2006

Hawken, Paul, Lovins Amory and Lovins L. Hunter, Natural Capitalism, Little Brown and Company, 1999

Heinberg Richard, The Party's Over, Oil, War and the Fate of Industrial Societies, 2003

Heinberg Richard, Peak Everything waking up to a century of decline, New Society Publishers, 2007

Heskett L. James, Sasser Earl W. Jr., Schlesinger A. Leonard, The Value Profit Chain, Free Press, 2003

Holland Nathan, A guide to Software Package Evaluation and Selection, AMACOM, 2000

Horner C. Christopher, Red Hot Lies, Regnery, 2008

Hulme, Mike, Why We Disagree About Climate Change, Cambridge University Press, 2009

Humes, Edward, Eco Barons, Ecco, 2009

Kaplan, S. Robert and Norton, P. David, The Balanced Scorecard, HBS Press, 1996

Lewis Bernard, What Went Wrong, The Clash Between Islam and Modernity in the Middle East, Perennial, 2002

Liker, Jeffrey K. The Toyota Way Fieldbook, New Tor: McGraw-Hill, 2006,

_____. *Toyota Talent: Developing People the Toyota Way.* New York: McGraw-Hill, 2007.

Lomberg, Global Crisies (Cambridge University Press), 2009.

Lovelock James, The Vanishing Face of Gaia A Final Warning, Allen Lane, 2009

Marks Susan J., Aqua Shock, Bloomberg, 2009

Mitchell Alanna, Sea Sick The Global Oceans in Crisis, Emblem, 2009

Michaels J. Patrick and Balling C. Robert Jr., Climate of Extremes, 2009

Mintzberg, Ahlstrand Bruce and Lampel Joseph, Strategy Safari A Guided Tour Through the Wilds of Strategic Management, Free Press, 1998

Nisbett E. Richard, The Geography of Thought, 2003

Patel Raj, The Value of Nothing (Harper Collins), 2009.

Patten Chris, What Next? Surviving the Twenty First Century, Viking Canada, 2009

Paskal Cleo, Global Warring, Key Porter Books 2009

Porter E. Michael, Competitive Strategy, The Free Press, 1980

Raynor E. Michael, The Strategy Paradox, Currency Doubleday 2007

Rhodes David and Stelter Daniel, Accelerating Out of the Great Recession, McGrawHill, 2010

Roberts Paul, The End of Food, Mariner, 2009

Rubin Jeff, Why Your World is About to Get a Whole Lot Smaller, Random House Canada, 2009

Sachs D. Jeffrey, Common Wealth Economics for a Crowded Planet, Penguin, 2008

Schonberger J. Richard, Let's Fix It, Free Press, 2001

Sirota David, Mischkind A. Louis and Meltzer Irwin Michael, The Enthusiastic Employee, Wharton School Publishing, 2005

Solomon Lawrence, The Deniers, Richard Vigilante Books, 2010

Srinivasan, M. Mandyam, Streamlined 14 Principles for Building & Managing The Lean Supply Chain, 2004

Steffen Alex ed. World Changinf, A User's Guide For the 21st Century, ABRAMS, 2009

Stiglitz E. Joseph, Freefall, Norton, 2010

Stiglitz E. Joseph, Making Globalization Work, Norton, 2007

Stringer Leigh, The Green Workplace, Palgrave Macmillan, 2009

Sullivan Malcolm and Adcock, Retail Marketing, Thomson, 2002

Van Jones, The Green Collar Economy, 2009

Weaver Andrew, Keeping Our Cool, Penguin Canada, 2008

Womack P. James and Jones T. Daniel, Lean Thinking, 1996

Notes

1. Jim Collins, *Good To Great: Why Some Companies Make the Leap … and Others Don't* (New York: Harper Business, 2001).
2. Sydney Finkelstein, *Why Smart Executives Fail* (New York: Portfolio 2003).
3. Daniel Goleman, *Ecological Intelligence* (New York: Broadway Books, 2009).
4. John Roach, "Are Plastic Grocery Bags Sacking the Environment?," *National Geographic* , September 2, 2003, http://news.nationalgeographic.com/news/2003/09/0902_030902_plasticbags.html.
5. Kagan Ryan, "How to Implement a Paperless Office," *CheckMark*, Autumn 2009, page 31 to 33.
6. Van Jones, *The Green Collar Economy* (New York: HarperCollins Publishers, 2009).
7. Bernard Lewis, *What Went Wrong?* (New York: Perennial, 2002).
8. Richard E. Nisbett, *The Geography of Thought* (New York: Free Press, 2003).
9. Ibid.
10. Ibid.
11. Rayne Kruger, *All under Heaven: A complete History of China* (Chichester, West Sussex, England: John Wiley & Sons Ltd., 2003), 299.
12. Joe Studwell, *The China Dream* (New York: Grove Press, 2002), 41.
13. Ibid., 45.
14. Alan De Brauw and John Giles, "Rural to Urban Migration in China: How Do Migrant-Sending Communities Benefit?" *World Bank*, April 8, 2008, http://go.worldbank.org/E3EOUMX661. See Cai Fang, Albert Park, and Yaohui Zhao, "The Chinese Labor Market in the Reform Era," in *China's Great Economic Transformation*, ed. Loren Brandt and Thomas G. Rawski, 167–214 (Cambridge: Cambridge University Press, 2007). The 2006 estimate

of the migrant population is drawn from the 2006 agricultural census, and reflects the number of migrants living outside their home counties for more than one month during the year.

15. Ibid.

16. Leslie Lipschitz, Céline Rochon, and Geneviève Verdier. "A Real Model of Transitional Growth and Competitiveness in China," working paper (IMF, 2008), http://www.ihs.ac.at/vienna/resources/Economics/Papers/20100225_Rochon_Paper.pdf.

17. Ellen Shell Ruppel, *Cheap* (New York: The Penguin Press, 2009), 214.

18. Ibid., 228.

19. ISBU, http://www.isbu-info.org/all_about_shipping_containers.html (Feb, 2010).

20. Ruppel, *Cheap*.

21. Ibid.

22. World Shipping Council Partners in Trade, May 2008, http://www.worldshipping.org/pdf/WSC_fuel_statement_final.pdf.

23. International Shipping News, August 28, 2009, http://internationalshippingnews.blogspot.com/2009/08/hapag-lloyd-financial-problems-as.html.

24. Ibid., 72.

25. Robert Fogel, "$123,000,000,000,000," *Foreign Policy,* Jan/Feb 2010, http://www.foreignpolicy.com/articles/2010/01/04/123000000000000.

26. Jack Goldstone, "The New Population Bomb," *Foreign Affairs,* Feb 2010, http://www.foreignaffairs.com/articles/65735/jack-a-goldstone/the-new-population-bomb.

27. Kathleen Kingsbury, "The Value of a Human Life," *Time*, May 20, 2008, http://www.time.com/time/health/article/0,8599,1808049,00.html.

28. David A.Farenthold , "Cosmic Markdown: EPA Says Life Is Worth Less," *Washington Post,* Saturday, July 19, 2008, page A01.

29. Raj Patel, *The Value of Nothing* (New York: Harper Collins, 2009), 18.

30. Ibid., 16.

31. Greenview, Conflict Conservation. *The Economist*, February 2010, Feb 13-19th

32. Steven Milloy, *Green Hell* (Washington DC: Regnery, 2009).

33. Chalmers Johnson, *Blowback: The Costs and Consequences of American Empire* (New York: Owl Books, 2000).

34. Paul Hawken, Amory Lovins, and L. Hunter Lovins, *Natural Capitalism* (New York: Back Bay Books, 1999).

35. Malcolm Sullivan and Dennis Adcock, *Retail Marketing* (New York: Thomson, 2002).

36. Hawken, Lovins, and Lovins, *Natural Capitalism*, 4.

37. Proverbs 29:18, *King James Bible*.

38. David Rhodes and Daniel Stelter, *Accelerating Out of the Great Recession* (New York: McGraw Hill, 2010), 4.

39. U.S. Bureau of Labor Statistics, http://www.bls.gov/cps/ (March).

40. U.S. Bureau of Labor Statistics, http://www.bls.gov/cps/ (March).

41. Don Peck, "How a Jobless Era Will Transform America," *The Atlantic*, March 2010.

42. Ibid.

43. Nicholas A. Christakis and James H. Fowler, *Connected* (New York: Little Brown and Company, 2009).

44. Chris Hails, "WWF Living Planet Report 2008," *Living Planet 2008 Report* (Gland, Switzerland: WWF International, 2008), 2.

45. World Atlas, http://www.worldatlas.com/ (March,2010).

46. "The World's Most Polluted Places," *Time* (June and 2010), http://www.time.com/time/specials/packages/completelist/0,29569,1661031,00.html

47. Stephen Leahy, "Tight Controls Could Save Global Fisheries," IPS, http://ipsnews.net/news.asp?idnews=47912.

48. E. Michael Raynor, *The Strategy Paradox* (New York: Broadway Business, 2007), 209–210.

49. Ibid., 210.

50. Ibid., 193.

51. Ellsworth Huntington, *Civilization and Climate* (Boston: University Press of the Pacific, 1915).

52. Fourth IPCC Report, February 2007, section 1.1.

53. Jeb Brugmann, *Welcome to the Urban Revolution: How Cities Are Changing the World* (New York: Bloomsbury Publishing PLC, 2009), 11.

54. National Geographic Society, "Freshwater Crisis," *National Geographic*, March, 2010 http://environment.nationalgeographic.com/environment/freshwater/freshwater-crisis.

55. Karl Russell, "Toxic Waters," a seven-part series, *New York Times*, Sept. 13, 2009.

56. Michael Blastland, "," BBC, April 20, 2009, http://browse.guardian.co.uk/search?search=Michael+Blastland%2C+&No=10&search_target=%2Fsearch&fr=cb-guardian.

57. Dickson Despommier, "The Rise of Vertical Farms," *Scientific American*, November 2009, http://www.scientificamerican.com/article.cfm?id=the-rise-of-vertical-farms.

58. MM&D Staff, "GS1 and VICS Introduce Empty Miles to Canada," February 17, 2010, http://www.canadianmanufacturing.com/mmd/news/supplychainnews/article.jsp?content=20100217_123856_11372.

59. Leigh Stringer, *The Green Workplace* (New York: Palgrave Macmillon, 2009).

60. Apple Inc.., "The Story Behind Apple's Environmental Footprint," http://www.apple.com/environment/complete-lifecycle/#undefined.

61. Joseph Goodman, Melissa Laube, and Judith Schwenk, "Curitiba's Bus System is Model for Rapid Transit," http://www.urbanhabitat.org/node/344.

62. Stringer, *The Green Workplace*, 48.

63. Scott Lee Walmart, "Wal-Mart CEO Lee Scott Unveils "Sustainability 360"," http://walmartstores.com/pressroom/news/6237.aspx.

64. Enwave, http://www.enwave.com/dlwc.php.

65. Plug Power Inc., http://www.plugpower.com.

66. Stringer, *The Green Workplace*.

67. Apple Inc.., "The Story Behind Apple's Environmental Footprint," http://www.apple.com/environment/complete-lifecycle/

68. Mark Schapiro, *Conning the Climate* (New York: Harpers, 2010).

69. Garth Hallberg, *All Consumers Are Not Created Equal* (New York: John Wiley & Sons, 1995).

70. "Greenspan admits 'mistake' that helped crisis," Associated Press updated 1:47 pm CT, Thurs., Oct. 23, 2008.

71. Ibid.

72. Joseph E. Stiglitz, *Freefall: America, Free Markets and the Sinking of World Economy* (New York: W. W. Norton & Company, 2010).

73. Samuel Bowles and Herbert Gintis, "Walrasian Economics in Retrospect," Department of Economics, University of Massachusetts, Amherst, Massachusetts, http://www.umass.edu/economics/publications/econ2000_04.pdf.

74. Stiglitz, *Freefall: America, Free Markets and the Sinking of World Economy*, 243.

75. International Operative Secretariat, "What is La Via Campesina?," http://viacampesina.org/en/index.php?option=com_content&view=category&layout=blog&id=27&Itemid=45.

76. Joseph E. Stiglitz, *Making Globalization Work* (New York: W.W. Norton & Company, 2006), 181.

77. Susan J. Marks, *Aqua Shock: The Water Crisis in America* (New York: Bloomberg Press, 2009), 188.

78. Amnesty.org, "Clouds of Injustice, Bhopol Disaster, 20 years on," (the link does not work) http://www.amnesty.org/en/library/info/ASA20/015/2004.

79. James Lovelock, *The Vanishing Face of Gaia: A Final Warning* (New York: Basic Books, 2009), 36.

80. Bjorn Lomberg, *Global Crisis, Global Solutions* (Cambridge: Cambridge University Press, 2009), 26.

81. Hawken, Lovins, and Lovins, *Natural Capitalism*, 4.

82. Paul Roberts, *The End of Food* (New York: Houghton Mifflin Harcourt, 2008), 70–77.

83. Rhodes and Stelter, *Accelerating Out of the Great Recession*, 38.

84. Ibid.

85. Corporate Sustainability Reporting Individuals like Paul Hawken (http://www.naturalcapitalism.org) and organizations such as the World Business Council for Sustainable Development (http://www.wbcsd.ch) have worked to publicize the economic, social, and environmental benefits associated with operating more sustainably. Reporting on achievements in this area can enhance a company's public image, but it also presents an opportunity for locating costly waste and inefficiency.

86. Amy Chua, *World On Fire: How Exporting Free Market Democracy Breeds Ethnic Hatred and Global Instability* (New York: Doubleday, 2003), 260.

87. Ibid.

88. Fareed Zakaria, *The Future of Freedom: Illiberal Democracy at Home and Abroad* (New York: W. W. Norton & Company, 2003), 13.

89. Ibid., 17.

90. Robert W. McChesney, *Rich Media, Poor Democracy: Communication Politics in Dubious Times* (Chicago: University of Illinois Press, 1999), 4–5.

91. Chua, *World On Fire*, 18.

92. Michel Chossudovsky, *War and Globalisation: The Truth Behind September 11th* (New York: Global Outlook, 2002).

93. Jean-Charles Brisard and Guillaume Dasquie, *Forbidden Truth, U.S.-Taliban Secret Oil Diplomacy and the failed hunt for Bin Laden* (New York: Nation Books, 2002), p.18.

94. Chua, *World On Fire*, 133.

95. Bradford D. Smart, *Topgrading: How Leading Companies Win by Hiring, Coaching and Keeping the Best People* (New York: Prentice Hall Press, 1999).

96. James Hoggan, *Climate Cover-Up* (Vancouver: Greystone Books, 2009).

97. Milloy, *Green Hell*.

98. Christopher C. Horner, *Red Hot Lies: How Global Warming Alarmists use Threats, Fraud, and Deception to Keep You Misinformed* (Washington DC: Regnery Publishing, Inc., 2008).

99.   Science and Technology, "Monitoring Greenhouse Gases: Highs and Lows," *The Economist*, March 6, 2010.

100. Ibid., 143–146.

101. The Equator Principles, http://www.equator-principles.com/documents/Equator_Principles.pdf.

102. Steve J. Stein and Howard Book, *The EQ Edge: Emotional Intelligence and Your Success* (Mississauga: John Wiley & Sons, 2001).

103. Goleman, *Ecological Intelligence*.

104. Hawken, Lovins, and Lovins, *Natural Capitalism*.

105. Jeffery K. Liker and Michael Hoseus, *Toyota Culture: The Heart and Soul of the Toyota Way* (New York: McGraw-Hill, 2008), 52.

106. David Sirota, Louis Mischkind, and Michael Irwin Meltzer, *The Enthusiastic Employee: How Companies Profit by Giving Workers What They Want* (New Jersey: Wharton School Publishing, 2005), 140.

107. Ibid., 141.

108. Mark A. Husefield, Bruce E. Becker, and Richard W. Beatty, *The Workforce Scorecard: Managing Human Capital to Execute Strategy* (Massachusetts: Harvard Business School Publishing, 2005), 35.

109. Rhodes and Stelter, *Accelerating Out of the Great Recession*, 91.

110. Henry Mintzberg, Joseph Lampel, and Bruce Ahlstrand, *Strategy Safari: A Guided Tour Through the Wilds of Strategic Management* (New York: Free Press, 1998).

111. Michael E. Porter, *Competitive Strategy: Techniques for Analyzing Industries and Competitors* (New York: Free Press, 1980), 35.

112. Ibid., 38.

113. James Cowan and Jacqueline Nelson, "How IBM went from selling stuff to selling ideas," *Canadian Business*, April 2010.

114. Robert S. Kaplan and David P. Norton, *The Balanced Scorecard: Translating Strategy into Action* (New Yotk: Harvard Business Press, 1996).

115. Dee Jacob, Suzan Bergland, and Jeff Cox, *Velocity, Combining Six Sigma and the Theory of Constraints in Achieving Breakthrough Performance* (New York: Free Press, 2009).

116. World Shipping Council Partners in Trade, May 2008, http://www.worldshipping.org/pdf/WSC_fuel_statement_final.pdf.

117. Justin Menkes, *Executive Intelligence, What All Great Leaders Have* (New York: HarperCollins, 2005), 68.

118. Ananth Ivyer, Sridhar Seshadri, and Roy Vasher, *Toyota Supply Chain Management: A Strategic Approach to Toyota's Renowned System* (New York: Mcgraw Hill, 2009), 3.

119. Ibid., 3

120. David D. Bedworth and James E. Bailey, *Integrated Production Control Systems, Management, Analysis Design* (New York: John Wiley & Sons, 1982).

121. Davis Guggenheim, *An Inconvenient Truth* (Los Angelos publisher, 2006), documentary film.

122. Ibid.

123. Huntington, *Title*.

124. Fourth IPCC Report, section 1.1.

125. Roy W. Spenser is a Principal Research Scientist at the University of Alabama in Huntsville and was formerly a Senior Scientist for Climate Studies at NASA.

126. Roy W. Spenser, *Climate Confusion: How Global Warming Hysteria Leads to Bad Science, Pandering Politicians and Misguided Policies that Hurt the Poor* (New York: Encounter Books, 2008), 67.

127. Fourth IPCC Report, section 1.1.

128. M. Pidwirny, "Atmospheric Composition," *Fundamentals of Physical Geography, 2nd* edition, http://www.physicalgeography.net/fundamentals/7a.html (March, 2010).

129. Water Vapor NASA Earth Observatory. http://www.nasa.gov/topics/earth/features/vapor_warming.html, March

130. Aerosols NASA Earth Observatory. http://www.nasa.gov/centers/langley/news/factsheets/Aerosols.html, March

131. U.S. Energy Information Administration.

132. Peter H. Spitz, *Petrochemicals: The Rise of An Industry* (New York: John Wiley & Sons, 1988), 235.

133. Daniel Yergin, *The Prize: The Epic Quest for Oil, Money, and Power* (New York: Free Press, 1993), 28.

134. Ibid., 371.

135. Ibid., 541.

136. Richard Heinberg, *The Party's Over: Oil, War and the Fate of Industrial Societies* (Gabriola Island, BC: New Society Publishers, 2003), 84.

137. Stephen Schwartz, *The Two Faces of Islam: The House of Sa'ud from Tradition to Terror* (New York: Double Day, 2002), 111.

138. A forerunner of ChevronTexaco.

139. Yergin, *The Prize*, 559.

140. Ibid., 629.

141. Ibid., 587.

142. Ibid., 779.

143. Heinberg, *The Party's Over*, 119.

144. Ibid., 93.

145. Thomas Homer-Dixon, *Carbon Shift: How the Twin Crises of Oil Depletion and Climate Change Will Define the Future* (New York: Random House Canada, 2009), 7.

146. Ibid., 8.

147. Source: U.S. Energy Information Administration,

148. Basra and Umm Qasr, "Iraq, Iran and the politics of oil Crude diplomacy," *The Economist*, February 2010.

149. Jeff Rubin, *Why Your World Is About to Get a Whole Lot Smaller* (Toronto: Random House Canada, 2009).

150. Leonard Maugeri, "Squeezing More Oil from the Ground," *Scientific American,* October 2008.

151. Ibid.

152. International Energy Agency 2009 Report Presentation to the press, http://www.iea.org/papers/2009/mtomr2009.pdf.

153. Rubin, *Why Your World,* 33.

154. Syncrude Canada Ltd., http://www.syncrude.ca/users/folder.asp?FolderID=5657.

155. Ibid., 62.

156. Katie Howell, "The Future of Oil Is in Deep Water," *Scientific American,* March 24, 2009.

157. U.S. Department of the Interior, Deepwater Gulf of Mexico 2009: Interim Report of 2008 Highlights.

158. Ibid.

159. Rubin, *Why Your World,* 49.

160. National Geographic Society, "Freshwater Crisis," *National Geographic,* http://environment.nationalgeographic.com/environment/freshwater http://environment.nationalgeographic.com/environment/freshwater/freshwater-crisis.

161. Maude Barlow, *Blue Covenant: The Global Water Crisis and the Coming Battle for the Right to Water* (Toronto: McClelland & Stewart, 2007).

162. U.S. Geological Survey 2005, .

163. USGS Sustainability of Ground Water Resources Study 1999, Circular 1186, http://pubs.usgs.gov/circ/circ1186/pdf/circ1186.pdf.

164. Russel, "Toxic Waters."

165. Marks, *Aqua Shock,* 14.

166. Zmarak Shalizi, Development Research Group, World Bank, Addressing China's Growing Water Shortages and Associated Social and Environmental Consequences, http://go.worldbank.org/Y87CX60TH0.

167. Alanna Mitchell, *Seasick: The Global Ocean in Crisis* (Toronto: McClelland & Stewart Ltd., 2009), 62.

168. Blastland, "Title."

169. Dickson Despommier, "The Rise of Vertical Farms."

170. World Population Growth:1950-2050US Census Bureau, Dec 2009, update, http://www.census.gov/ipc/www/idb/worldpopgraph.php (accessed June 12, 2010)

171. Nigel Key and Michael J. Roberts, "Measures of Trends in Farm Size Tell Differing Stories," November 2007, http://www.ers.usda.gov/AmberWaves/November07/DataFeature/.

172. Bryan McMurry, "Cow Size is Growing," BeefMagazine.com, .

173. Andy W. Speedy, "Global Consumption of Animal Source Foods," 2003 The American Society for Nutritional Sciences J. Nutr. 133:4048S-4053S, November 2003.

174. Cast Council for Agriculture and Science and Technology, July 1999,

175. International Food Policy Research Institute, "Rising Food Prices Threaten World's Poor," December 4, 2007,

176. "The Brown Lagoon," *The Economist,* November 22, 2009.

177. Stephen Goetz, Viney P. Aneja, and Yang Zhang. "Article: Measurement, analysis, and modeling of fine particulate matter in eastern North Carolina. (TECHNICAL PAPER) (Technical report)," from *Journal of the Air & Waste Management Association*, September 1, 2008, accessed through HighBeam Research, http://www.highbeam.com/doc/1G1-185952890.html.

178. James 2:14–15, *New King James Bible.*

Author Bio

CHRIS PROVOST has delivered over two hundred million in net profit growth for companies -- by improving their business value chain, supply chain and logistics processes. He has negotiated with hundreds of organizations in his leadership roles as Director of Fleet, Strategy & Shared Services and Director of National Transportation at Walmart; leadership roles with Unilever and other major brands. A Value Chain expert with extensive experience in Supply Chain, Logistics, Systems, Manufacturing, Financial management and Marketing; Chris has also ran major projects for a government corporation.